HOME
DECORATING

© Haynes Publishing 1997 and 2010
Reprinted in paperback June 2015

All rights reserved. No part of this publication may be reproduced, stored in a
retrieval system or transmitted, in any form or by any means, electronic, mechanical,
photocopying, recording or otherwise, without prior permission in writing from the
publisher.

Published by: Haynes Publishing
Sparkford, Yeovil, Somerset BA22 7JJ

British Library Cataloguing-in-Publication Data: A catalogue record for this book is
available from the British Library.

ISBN 978 0 85733 837 2

Printed in the USA by Odcombe Press LP,
1299 Bridgestone Parkway, La Vergne, TN 37086

Authors: Julian Cassell, Peter Parham, Alex Portelli

Photography: James Merrell, Nick Pope, Tim Ridley, Debi Treloar, Polly Wreford,
                  George Wright

Illustration: David Eaton, Fred van Deelen

Page layout: Dominic Stickland

While every effort is taken to ensure the accuracy of the information given in this
book, no liability can be accepted by the author or the publisher for any loss,
damage or injury caused by errors in, or omissions from, the information given.

*This book has been compiled, adapted and updated from four books originally
published by Haynes in 1997:* Painting Your Home: Interiors, The Wallpapering
Book, The Wall Tiling Book *and* Painting Your Home: Exteriors.

HOME DECORATING

Covers all rooms, surfaces, styles and techniques

Contents

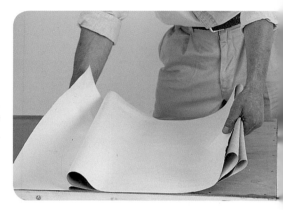

CHAPTER 2

CHAPTER 3

CHAPTER 4

Introduction

Redecorating your home, as well as helping to maintain the fabric of the property, allows you to capitalise on the most attractive features of your house and gives you the opportunity to create a particular style or look. When contemplating redecoration, most people have ideas, perhaps influenced by images they have seen in magazines, about the styles that they like, but are often unsure how to translate these to their own homes. This book, which is written by professional decorators, explains the fundamental principles underlying successful home decoration. It breaks down a wide variety of decorating projects into manageable stages, with easily followed instructions and clear step-by-step colour photographs explaining each step in the process. Giving ideas on colour choices and details of the tools and materials that you will need, as well as comprehensive information on how to undertake the task itself, the book is designed to take the mystery out of even seemingly complex home decorating jobs.

PAINTING INTERIORS

Repainting a room instantly lifts it, and with a wide variety of paints available at moderate prices, a revamp of the interior of your home need not cost the earth. The most difficult decisions when painting interiors often lie in choosing colours and finishes. Inspiration may not come immediately, so use all available 'props' to help with decision-making. Most paint manufacturers provide tester pots and colour swatches with which you can experiment. Look through magazines for a room or style that catches your attention. Above all remember that your personal taste and requirements are the most important factors.

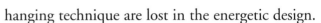

WALLPAPERING

With an almost unlimited variety of patterns and textures available, modern papers offer the decorator great flexibility. With a careful choice of colour and pattern, wallpapers can be used to flatter the most attractive features in a room and disguise any minor flaws. Large patterns tend to be the most dramatic and are usually most effective in large rooms. Smaller, busy patterns create a more active impression in a room and provide an excellent backdrop for paintings, ornaments and general architectural features. These papers hide any imperfections in the surface and are generally easier for the beginner to hang, as small mistakes in paper-hanging technique are lost in the energetic design.

When selecting wallpaper, it is important to bear in mind the practicality of the paper for the room it is decorating. In a bathroom, for example, a paper which can withstand the high levels of condensation and moist atmosphere should be used (vinyl papers are ideal, as their washable coating protects them from the damp and keeps them clean). Likewise, a durable paper, able to withstand continual wiping down and general cleaning should be used in a kitchen. Some wallpapers are particularly delicate and should therefore not be used in areas, like a children's bedroom or playroom, where hard-wearing characteristics are required.

WALL TILING

Wall tiles, which have been popular for centuries, provide a hard-wearing, waterproof surface that is both decorative and functional. There is a wealth of wall tiles from which to choose and as a result, no matter what the style of decor, you should be able to find the right tiles for the job. In rooms with old-fashioned fittings, tiles in subdued tones create a pleasing, but unobtrusive backdrop. Modern fittings with chromium-plated or stainless steel accessories are complemented by black and white tiles, which suggest an air of luxury and style.

Take your time when deciding on a tiling scheme; wall tiles are not only more expensive than other forms of decoration, but they are also more difficult to change if you are not happy with them. It is essential to find a scheme that you can live with for a long time. If in doubt, opt for something simple that will provide a neutral backdrop rather than a design that will become a major visual feature. You may find inspiration in magazines, other people's homes, tile brochures, displays at tile suppliers, or even the patterns in wallpapers or fabrics.

EXTERIOR PAINTING

Choosing colours and finishes is very much a matter of personal taste. However, there are certain issues of practicality and indeed occasional restrictions which must be considered. Maintaining the character of your home may be important, so be sure to consider the architecture and period influences before making drastic changes. Also, bear in mind that if your house is in a conservation area it may be subject to limits on colour choice.

The walls are the largest surfaces on a house and are therefore the most dominant aspect in the overall appearance of its exterior. Maintaining them properly and painting them regularly ensures that your house looks its best, and is properly protected from the damaging effects of harsh weather. Smooth render, painted white, is a safe but practical option, that provides a good backdrop for plants and garden accessories. Textured coating or paints are also practical, hard-wearing finishes.

Features such as doors, window frames, gutters and downpipes also need to be decorated. Depending on how attractive they are, they may be either highlighted, to accentuate a particular characteristic, or blended in, to camouflage a less appealing item. On properties which have little or no painted masonry, using bold colours on woodwork and metal fittings can add to the general appearance of a house.

Choosing colours

A basic understanding of how colours can be mixed, and how they interact is essential if you are to achieve the decorative effect that you want. The best way to ensure successful results is to prepare a number of colour samples and display them for a few days in the room to be decorated.

MIXING COLOURS

In theory all colours can be created from the three primaries, blue, yellow and red, together with black and white. The example (right), which blends together three glazes mixed with primary bases, illustrates how the primary colours blend and how difficult it is to achieve colours with true vibrance and purity. But manufacturers now produce such vast colour ranges that mixing can be limited to adjusting ready-mixed colours.

Using the colour wheel
When combining colours for colour schemes these are three simple rules to follow to ensure successful results.

Complementary colours
Colours on opposite sides of the colour wheel are known as complementary colours because together they create a full complement of all the spectral hues. Each is the other's strongest possible contrast, showing it up most vividly, as when oranges are wrapped in blue or purple tissue, or butchers decorate a window display with green leaves.

Closely related colours
Colours that appear next to each other on the colour wheel are closely related and always blend well with one another. However, a scheme made up only of closely-related colours lacks the zing that contrasts introduce.

Harmonizing colours
Three colours equidistant on the colour wheel will harmonize with each other.

Reducing colour strength

When two complementary colours are mixed they produce a grey midtone. This can be usefully exploited when mixing colours. If a colour is too vibrant the addition of its complementary colour produces a less vibrant, but still clean, colour. White reduces colour strength to produce a tint while retaining its purity.

Creating a balanced scheme

The intensity of a colour is a measure of how dull or vivid it is, while its value measures how dark or light it is. A balanced scheme is one in which no one colour used overpowers the others. It is as important to use colours of similar intensity and value as it is to co-ordinate them.

Colour clarity is impaired by adding black

Colour value is reduced and made lighter by adding white

Mixed complementary colours produce grey midtones

THE EFFECT OF LIGHT ON COLOUR

Artificial light

Light affects the appearance of colours. In yellowish artificial light, blue may seem green.

Natural daylight

It is important to check colours you intend to use in both natural daylight and artificial light.

COLOUR COMBINATIONS

To devise successful colour schemes, take note of the colours used in a room that particularly appeals to you and also look at how colour combinations work in nature. Always remember that a room's decorations should act as a backdrop to your treasured possessions rather than overpower them.

Using colour cleverly

Choice of the right colour scheme can considerably enhance a room, changing both its atmosphere and its apparent shape. Is the room light or dark, sunny or cold? Is it long and thin, or perhaps small yet high-ceilinged? What is its use? Take all these considerations into account when making colour choices, for choices based on improving aspect as well as simply on colour preference determine the success or failure of a scheme. Careful planning removes the element of chance, ensuring a successful end result.

CHOOSING THE STYLE

Manufacturers produce a wide variety of paints and papers, providing a wealth of colours, styles and textures from which to choose. But this very choice, and the flexibility it gives you, can be a source of bewilderment, making it quite hard to know where to begin.

As a start, some key decorators' principles are illustrated in the drawings on this and the opposite page. These show the effect of colours that are dark and light, warm and cold, and also how patterns of different kinds can affect the apparent shape and size of a room.

The first stage of planning a colour scheme for decorating a whole room – before you begin to test out colour samples – can be done on paper. Take a photograph of the room you intend to decorate, then make several photocopies of it. Colouring in the photocopies in your possible schemes will soon show up any problems and help you to decide which scheme will be the most effective.

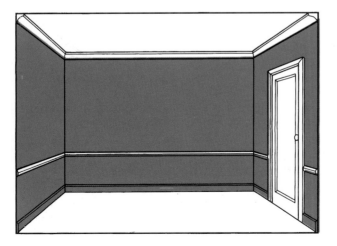

A warm colour draws a surface towards you and can create a cosy effect.

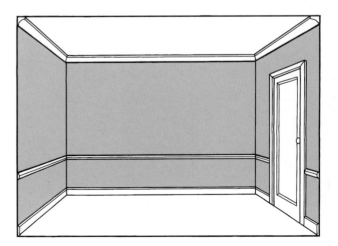

A cool colour takes the surface away from you and creates an impression of space.

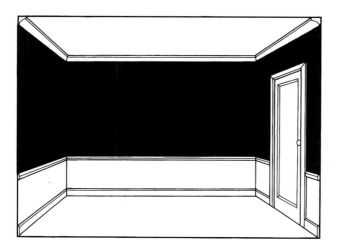

A dark colour draws a surface towards you and can make the ceiling appear lower.

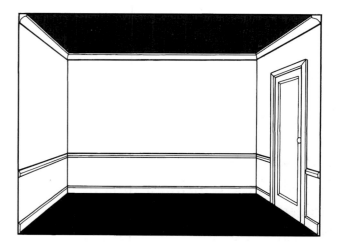

Using both a dark floor colour and a dark ceiling colour draws the two surfaces together.

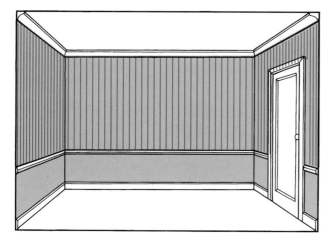

Vertical stripes draw the eye upwards and therefore appear to heighten a room.

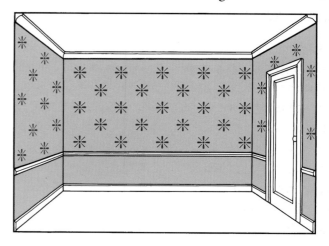

Large patterns bring walls towards you and can be used to best effect in large rooms.

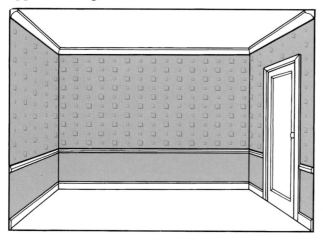

Small patterns, like cool colours, create an illusion of space.

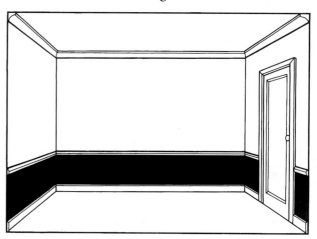

Darker colour on the lower walls encloses the space; a light area above creates an illusion of space.

Tools

When choosing and purchasing tools and equipment, always opt for quality rather than quantity. A few well-selected, superior items will be far more useful than buying cheap 'all-in-one' kits. These often contain many articles that you will never use.

When assembling tools, it is not necessary to purchase the complete range as listed here. Instead, buy for your specific needs and build up your equipment gradually. Also, if you have limited use for an item, especially the more expensive ones such as steam strippers, it may be more sensible to consider hiring rather than making an outright purchase.

BASIC TOOLBOX FOR PREPARATION

Slot-head screwdrivers

Cross-head screwdrivers

Scraper
A broad, rigid blade for removing old paint and paper finishes.

Filling knife
A flexible blade helps to push filler into cracks and holes.

Hammer

Pencil

Nail punch

Tape measure

Pliers

Plier wrench
Similar to pliers, but has an adjustable, locking head to get a good grip.

Wire brush
Removes loose paint when repairing metal.

Filler dispenser
A universal frame that can take a variety of filler and sealant tubes.

Dusting brush

Plumb line
Indicates an exact vertical.

Chalk line
Marks a long, straight line where distance is too long for a steel rule.

Spirit level

Steel rule

Chisels

Float

Trowel

Hawk

Masking tape
Protects adjoining areas when working. Also prevents drill bit from skidding when drilling tiles.

Bucket

Sponge

Electric drill

Access and personal protection

Step-ladder

Dust sheet

Trestles and plank
Make a sturdy platform when working on ceilings or high walls.

Protective gloves
Waterproof, to keep irritants off hands.

Goggles
Keep dust, spray and chemicals out of eyes.

Dust masks
(disposable)

Respirator mask
Protection against very fine dust and fumes.

Stripping and sanding

Steam stripper
For fast wallpaper stripping.

Sand-, abrasive or glass paper

Electric hot-air gun
For stripping paint or varnish.

Electric sander
For large areas.

PAINTING TOOLS

Paint preparation

Lid opener

Stirring stick

Paint kettle

Paint and varnish brushes

Paintbrushes

Varnish brushes

Angle-headed paintbrush
Ideal for painting window bars and rebates.

Fitches
For detailed work.

Brush comb

Cleaning system box

Rollers, paint pads and sprayers

Roller cage and roller sleeves
Different sizes and textures of sleeve will fit on the same roller cage.

Roller tray

Corner roller

Paint pads

Airless sprayer

Airless spray gun

PAPER-HANGING TOOLS

Radiator roller

Paper-hanging brush

Paper-hanging scissors
Long blades help to cut straight edges.

Pasting brush

Measuring jug

Seam roller
Presses joins flat, when hanging paper.

Pasting table

Craft knife

Craft knife with snap-off blades

Fitch
For adding paste.

Wallpaper trough

TILING TOOLS

Grout shaper
Finishes grout joints neatly .

Small trowel
For scooping adhesive on to wall and grout on to tiles.

Sealant dispenser
Use when applying silicone sealant.

Notched adhesive spreader

Junior hacksaw
Cuts plastic corner trim and bath-sealing strip.

Grout spreader (squeegee)

Plastic scouring pad
Removes excess epoxy grout from worktop tiles.

Tile scorer/grout raker
For scoring tiles when cutting or removing old grout .

Tile-cutting tools

Tile spike
For scoring tiles when cutting.

Nibblers
Removes narrow strips or waste from intricate shapes.

Tile file
For cleaning up edges of tiles after cutting .

Tile-cutting machine
Measures, scores and cuts tiles.

Combined cutting wheel/snapper
Scores and snaps tiles.

Tile saw
Cuts intricate shapes or moulded tiles.

Caring for tools

Equipment should be cleaned thoroughly before being put away. Do not make the common mistake of leaving brushes in a jar of white spirit and expecting them to be as good as new in six months' time, as they will simply dry out and be ruined. There are obvious savings to be made by looking after expensive brushes and rollers. Although the process may seem arduous at the time, you will be grateful when you come to tackle the next decorating project.

Remember to dispose of any empty cans or chemical debris safely.

TOOLS: Scraper, sponge, craft knife

MATERIALS: Household detergent, white spirit, glass jar, clean cloth, brown paper, rubber band, hand cleanser

WATER-BASED PAINT

Clean brushes, rollers or pads by first wiping off the excess paint on some newspaper. Then wash the tool under running water with some mild detergent until the water runs clear. Rinse and shake dry. Draw a blunt scraper across the bristles, to remove dried paint from brushes.

SOLVENT-BASED PAINT

Remove any excess paint, then stir the brush vigorously in a jar of white spirit. Dry the brush thoroughly with a clean cloth. Repeat the process if paint is still evident in the bristles. Finally wash with warm water and detergent, rinse and shake dry.

CLEANING HANDS

Many decorating products may irritate the skin, so adequate protection, such as gloves, should always be worn. However, splashes of paint are sometimes unavoidable. To clean them off, use a proprietary hand cleanser.

WALLPAPER PASTE

Wash the paper-hanging brush under warm running water using household detergent to remove any dry paste. Rinse thoroughly and allow to dry before storing. To clean the pasting brush, remove as much excess paste as possible from the bristles, then wash, rinse and dry in the same way. Rinse the paper-hanging scissors in warm water under the tap, sponging off any dry paste, then dry with a clean cloth to prevent any possibility of corrosion.

PASTE DISPOSAL

Most wallpaper paste contains fungicide and so is not biodegradable. Therefore, paste should never be tipped down a drain, as it may pollute nearby streams. Put it in a sealed container before throwing it out.

CLEANING SYSTEM BOX

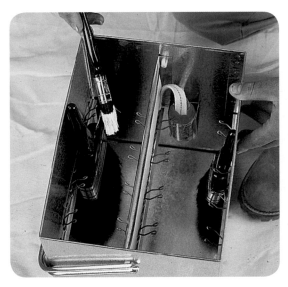

As an alternative to cleaning out brushes which have been used with solvent-based products, a proprietary cleaning-system box may be used. Brushes can be stored indefinitely by suspending the drying process. Chemical vapour contained in such an enclosed space allows the bristles to remain moist and ready for use.

CRAFT KNIVES

Before putting away a craft knife, it should be carefully wiped clean with a damp cloth, then dried thoroughly. Dispose of old blades – even if they are blunt – by placing them in a container such as an empty paint can. Make sure the can is sealed securely before putting it out with the rest of the rubbish.

STORAGE

All brushes should be dry before they are put away. In order to keep them in prime condition, wrap the bristles in brown paper held in place with a rubber band. This will help the brush to keep its shape rather than allowing the bristles to splay out in all directions.

CHAPTER 1

PAINTING INTERIORS

Whether you are a complete novice or have done some decorating before, this chapter contains all the information you need to paint the interior of your home.

There is a huge range of decorative products on the market and decision-making can be difficult. The opening pages of the chapter aim to help you to make the right choices, providing you with ideas on colour schemes and practical advice on types of paint.

Planning the work and taking time to carry it out in an ordered, logical manner will be amply rewarded, with the finish looking better and lasting for longer. All the information that you need to complete these essential preparatory stages is explained step by step, including details on how to strip paper, prime and fill surfaces, clean down, and hang lining paper prior to painting.

Finally, painting techniques are explained, teaching the principal methods of application and giving advice on the correct way to paint ceilings, walls, doors and windows.

Pale colours

Colours that are neutral and pale always give an impression of space because they reflect light more than darker colours. Rooms that do not receive much natural light can look airier when they have pale walls and ceilings, and some rooms may look less cluttered than they otherwise might.

The most common application of this principle is when ceilings are painted white to 'raise' the height of a room.

Pale colours also tend to be popular because it is easier to match furnishings with such neutral tones than with bolder, more vibrant ones.

◀ Pale pastel colours tend to be calming, and produce a relaxed, comfortable atmosphere. Shades of peach or apricot add warmth to this room. The pale slate blue provides a note of contrast, but because it is of a similar intensity to the wall colour, the overall tone is still restful.

◀ Pale hues provide perfect backdrops for favourite furnishings, ornaments or displays.

▲ Bright yellow, while not a neutral colour, adds life to what might otherwise be a dull, unwelcoming area. Other primary colours produce a similar effect in lifting the 'mood' of a room.

◀ Greens and blues are considered cool colours, providing a fresh yet soothing atmosphere. The lighter the shade, the more the walls will tend to recede, giving the impression of space.

Pictures or paintings will also stand out against a light background.

Dark colours

Dark colours are always a bold choice, but they can add considerable character to flat and lifeless surfaces and accentuate features within a room. Dark colours may create a slightly enclosed feeling, appearing to bring high ceilings down and making wall surfaces advance rather than recede. This effect can be used to create a cosy, relaxed feeling, especially in rooms used principally in the evening.

Dark colours may seem too daring for many of us. To counteract this, try using them on woodwork, so they will not be as overpowering as on a large wall surface. Furthermore, it is often wiser to use a colour one or two shades lighter than your original choice, as the colour will always seem darker once applied, especially on a large area.

▲ The deep brick red on the rear walls of the shelving complements the green perfectly, and creates a further dimension to the decoration.

◄ The dark forest green of this woodwork stands out magnificently against the pale yellow walls, emphasising the shape of the bookshelves and providing an ideal showcase for both ornaments and books.

◀ Dark blues are perceived to be cool colours which often steers people away from using them.

▼ Subtle lighting, however, may change the appearance of colours dramatically. Here, the blue on these walls displays this principle perfectly.

◀ Rich, dark red enhances the natural beauty of wood and adds a certain opulence to extravagant soft furnishings. By keeping the window bay white, the maximum amount of natural light is allowed into the room.

Interior paint finishes

Almost all paints suitable for the interior of houses can be divided into two broad categories: water-based and solvent-based. Water-based paints tend to be easier to use and are more environmentally friendly than solvent-based.

The types of paint that you choose and the order in which you apply them affect the final finish. The tables on these pages give guidance on the handling and application techniques for a number of paints.

GUIDE TO PAINT FINISHES

	PRODUCT DESCRIPTION	SUITABLE SURFACES	MAIN QUALITIES	LIMITATIONS	APPLICATION METHOD
PRIMER	Watery, dilute appearance specifically formulated to seal bare surfaces.	All bare wood, plaster or metal. Specific or all-purpose primers are available.	Excellent sealer enabling application of further coats of paint.	Only use on bare surfaces.	Brush. May use roller or spray with water-based primers.
PRIMER-UNDERCOAT	A primer and undercoat in one, providing base for top coat(s).	Bare wood.	Easy to use, and time-saving.	Not as hard-wearing as oil-based undercoat.	Brush, roller or spray.
UNDERCOAT	Dull, opaque finish providing ideal base for application of top coat(s).	Any primed surface.	Hard-wearing.	Application takes longer than primer-undercoat.	Brush or roller.
MATT EMULSION	All purpose matt-finish paint. Water–based.	Plaster surfaces.	A thinned first coat acts as an excellent primer. Apply full strength coats to finish.	Not hard-wearing.	Brush, roller or spray.
VINYL EMULSION	Available in a number of finishes from matt to silk. Water–based.	On primed or previously painted plaster surfaces, or direct to lining paper.	Vinyl qualities make it easy to clean.	When 'cutting in' with dark colours, framing effect difficult to avoid.	Brush, roller or spray.
EGGSHELL	Mid-sheen finishing paint. Proprietary variations on this theme.	Any primed or undercoated surface.	More hard-wearing than emulsions.	Slight sheen tends to accentuate imperfections on large surface areas.	Brush or roller; spray with water-based.
GLOSS	Shiny 'polished' finishing paint.	Any undercoated surface, ideally wood or metal.	Very hard-wearing decorative finish. Easy to clean.	Application is time consuming and requires a sound technique.	Brush or roller.
TEXTURED PAINT	Textured relief paint, that can be used as a finish or overpainted.	Plaster surfaces.	Adds further decorative dimension to flat walls or ceilings. Excellent for hiding rough surfaces.	Difficult to clean. Difficult to remove if redecoration required.	Roller, brush, combs/variety of finishing tools.

ORDER OF WORK

Water-based paint on new plaster
1 Bare plaster
2 Dilute matt-emulsion primer coat
3 First coat of finishing paint
4 Top coat of finishing paint Apply further coats if required

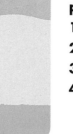

Water-based paint on lining paper
1 Bare plaster
2 PVA sealer or size
3 Lining paper
4 Finishing paint: two to three coats

Water-based paint on wood
1 Bare wood
2 Knotter on bare knots
3 Primer-undercoat
4 Second primer-undercoat for improved finish, or apply first coat of eggshell if top coat is going to be eggshell
5 Top coat: gloss or eggshell

Oil-based paint on wood
1 Bare wood
2 Knotter on bare knots
3 Primer
4 Undercoat: apply two coats for improved finish
5 Top coat: gloss
If using eggshell, apply two coats directly on top of primer; undercoat is not necessary

WATER-BASED vs SOLVENT-BASED: THE PROS AND CONS

	WATER-BASED	SOLVENT-BASED	COMMENTS
EASE OF APPLICATION	• • • • •	• • •	Water-based tend to be much easier to apply, with less 'brushing out' required.
DRYING TIME	• • • • •	•	Much quicker turn-around between coats with water-based paints.
LOW ODOUR/TAINT	• • • • •	•	White-spirit smell of solvent-based paints can be overpowering. Minimal problem with water-based.
WASHABILITY	• • •	• • • • •	Surfaces painted with solvent-based paints are easiest to clean.
DURABILITY	• • •	• • • • •	Solvent-based are more hard-wearing, although water-based are catching up with improved formulation.
BRUSHMARKS	• •	• • • •	More evident in water-based, although improving all the time.
COLOUR RETENTION	• • • •	• • •	White solvent-based (especially) tends to yellow with age.
CLEANING TOOLS	• • • • •	•	Water-based easily cleaned with water and mild detergent. Solvent-based is a lengthier process requiring white spirit.
USER-FRIENDLY	• • • •	•	All health and safety guidelines make water-based products a better option than their solvent-based counterparts.

Identifying problems

Before starting any preparation, the room must first be cleared of obstacles. It is best to remove all the furniture, accessories and soft furnishings, and to take up the carpet at this stage, if it is to be replaced. If it is not possible to clear the room totally, place everything in the middle and cover with dust sheets. You are now able to get a clear view of any problem areas, decide how to treat them and to assess the extent of redecoration required. The problems outlined below are commonplace in many homes. All of them need attention before any decoration is carried out.

DAMP AND MOULD

Mould is caused by moisture build-up, usually as a result of poor ventilation. Wash it down with fungicide. Extensive mould growth should be looked at by a professional as there may be a general damp problem that needs to be solved before redecoration can take place. Old stains, caused by damp that has dried out, can be covered with proprietary sealers.

CRACKED/CHIPPED WOODWORK

Results from general wear and tear. Depending on its extent, woodwork will need to be stripped totally or just filled and sanded before it is repainted (see pages 42–43).

WRINKLED PAPER

Commonly found in corners where the walls are not quite square and poor paper adhesion, plus slight movement in the building, has lifted and possibly torn the paper. Small areas can be cut out with a scraper, refilled and painted over.

BLEEDING KNOTS

Caused by resin weeping from a live knot, usually in relatively new timber. Strip back and seal (see pages 36–37).

POWDERY WALL SURFACES

Found in older houses that were previously painted with a type of paint called distemper, or may just be due to the breakdown of old plaster. Wash down and seal (see pages 44–45).

FLAKING TEXTURED FINISHES

Caused by water penetration (such as a burst pipe) or a poorly prepared surface. Small areas can be patched. With larger areas, the whole surface must be stripped back and the finish reapplied.

FLAKY PAINT

Caused by moisture underneath the painted surface, or where the paint has been unable to stick to a powdery or incompatible surface. (See left, and Sealing on pages 44–45.)

UNEVEN PAPERED SURFACES

Generally found in older properties. If the paper is basically sound or an overall 'rustic' finish is acceptable, do not strip as the plaster underneath may come away from the wall. Simply paint over the existing paper.

EFFLORESCENCE

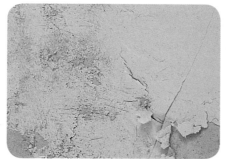

Results from crystallisation of salts found in building materials. Use a scraper to remove deposits until no more appear. Repaint with water-based paint, which allows drying out to continue through the painted surface.

LIFTING WALLPAPER SEAMS

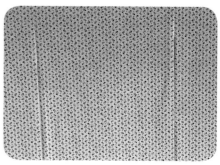

Caused by poor application, lack of paste adhesion due to damp, or simply ageing. Small areas of lining paper can be stuck back down with border adhesive. With larger areas, the whole room should be stripped and repapered.

BUBBLING PAPER

This is caused by inexpert papering or poor adhesion. The only solution is to strip and repaper the problem area (see pages 34–35).

CRACKS IN PLASTER

Caused by drying out, building settlement and general wear and tear. Fill and allow to dry out completely before painting or papering (see pages 38–39).

Paint and materials

When buying materials – and most importantly, paint – spending a little more on good-quality products will save both time and money in the long run. It is a false economy to apply four or five coats of a cheap paint when a slightly more expensive counterpart will do the job in two coats. Remember to be selective with your requirements for the particular job in hand, as many of the items on this page have only a limited shelf life.

BASIC SUPPLIES
Fillers

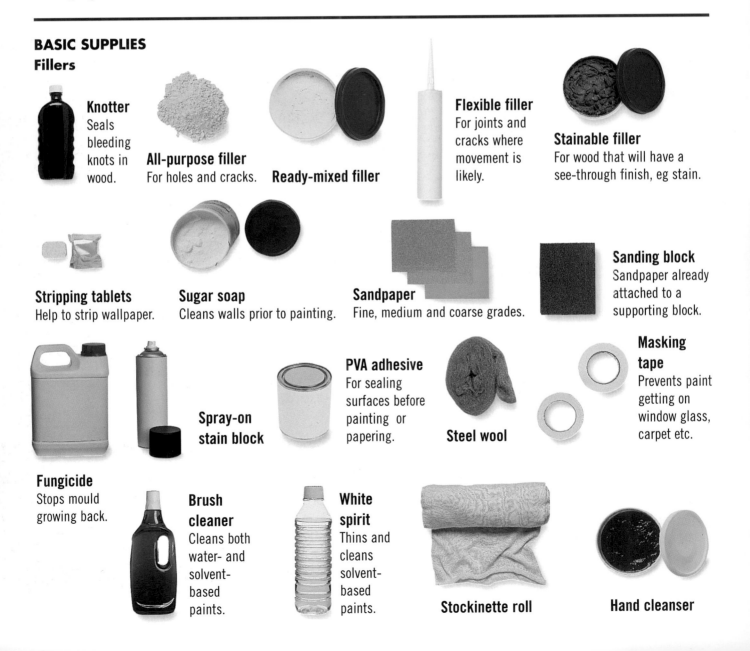

Knotter
Seals bleeding knots in wood.

All-purpose filler
For holes and cracks.

Ready-mixed filler

Flexible filler
For joints and cracks where movement is likely.

Stainable filler
For wood that will have a see-through finish, eg stain.

Stripping tablets
Help to strip wallpaper.

Sugar soap
Cleans walls prior to painting.

Sandpaper
Fine, medium and coarse grades.

Sanding block
Sandpaper already attached to a supporting block.

Spray-on stain block

PVA adhesive
For sealing surfaces before painting or papering.

Steel wool

Masking tape
Prevents paint getting on window glass, carpet etc.

Fungicide
Stops mould growing back.

Brush cleaner
Cleans both water- and solvent-based paints.

White spirit
Thins and cleans solvent-based paints.

Stockinette roll

Hand cleanser

LINING

Wallpaper paste

Lining paper
(see pages 48–49
for quantities)

Overlap adhesive
Stronger than ordinary paste.

Craft-knife blades
Replace often for a sharp
edge at all times.

FINISHING

Primer
Undercoat
Top coat: matt,
eggshell or gloss

Stain
Varnish
Wax
Oil
Wood dye

CAUTION
Some materials contain hazardous chemicals. Always remember to read the manufacturers' guidelines before handling them.

COVERAGE

To estimate quantities, it is first necessary to measure the various surface areas. Walls and ceilings are relatively straightforward, and the same method as used for measuring up for lining paper may be used (see pages 48–49).

When calculating how much paint is needed for a window, measure it as you would a door by multiplying the height by the width. Do not deduct the glass area as this will compensate for the intricate areas of the window which make its actual surface area larger than it would appear. (However, with picture windows a deduction should be made.)

The table on the right can only give an approximate guide to how much paint is needed as some surfaces are more porous than others. These figures are calculated for surfaces of average porosity. Each manufacturer will produce slight variations on coverage, so it is best to take their estimates into account when buying the paint.

ACRYLIC/WATER-BASED	sq m/litre	sq yd/gallon
Gloss	15	82
Eggshell	15	82
Emulsion	15	82
Primer/undercoat	12	65

SOLVENT-/OIL-BASED		
Gloss	17	92
Eggshell	16	87
Undercoat	15	82
Primer	13	71

Stripping paper

This is a time-consuming job, but with the correct methods it is reasonably straightforward. A steam stripper, which can be hired quite cheaply, speeds up the process. When using it, always wear rubber gloves and goggles as boiling water and steam can spit out from the sides of the stripping pad. If a steam stripper is not available, soak the paper with hot water or use a stripping-tablet solution instead. Gloves and goggles are still required as most stripping chemicals will irritate the skin.

TOOLS: Gloves, goggles, steam stripper, measuring jug, scraper, bucket, stirring stick, 130mm (5in) brush, wallpaper spiker or orbital scorer

MATERIALS: Stripping tablets, water

STEAM STRIPPING

1 When using a steam stripper always read the instructions. Check that the steam stripper is turned off at its power source, then pour water into its reservoir. Warm water will reduce the time needed for the stripper to boil. Then switch on the power and wait for the water to boil. Never leave a steam stripper unattended when it is switched on.

2 Put on your goggles and gloves. Place the stripper's steam pad firmly on the wallpaper you wish to strip, holding it in the same position, without moving, for about 30 seconds. Some brands of wallpaper stripper and some heavyweight papers may require a longer time for steaming.

3 Move the pad across the wall and using a scraper, strip off the loose, bubbling paper. Take care not to dig the end of the scraper into the wall, gouging holes in the plaster. You will soon build up a rhythm of stripping the paper with one hand while steaming the next piece of wall with the other.

STRIPPING WITH WATER

1 Measure hot water into a bucket and add the correct number of stripping tablets. Stir thoroughly until they are completely dissolved. Hot water alone can also be effective for soaking wallpaper.

2 Using a large brush, apply the solution to the paper, working from the top down. Do not soak more than a few square metres (yards) at a time or the paper will dry out before you have a chance to strip it off.

3 Allow the paper to soak for a few minutes, strip it away with a scraper. It is a good idea to clear up as you work, as otherwise the stripped paper will dry out on your dust sheets and become difficult to remove.

STRIPPING VINYL WALLPAPER

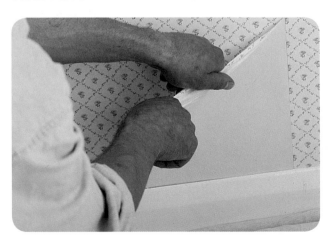

With vinyl papers, it may be possible to pull the top layer away from the backing paper, doing away with the need for a spiker/scorer. Never be tempted to leave the backing paper on the wall, however good its condition. It is rarely a sound surface on which to start decorating.

IDEAL TOOLS

Spiker

Orbital scorer

With all types of wallpaper, it is a good idea to run a wallpaper spiker or orbital scorer over the paper prior to soaking. There are several different types of spiker/scorer on the market, but all work in the same way: they aim to perforate the top layer, allowing moisture underneath the paper to aid the stripping process.

Priming and knotting

Priming is the first stage of painting a bare surface, be it wood, metal or plaster. (Plaster surfaces are covered on pages 44–45.) Primer provides a surface to which the following coats of paint can bond, making sure of even coverage. With wood especially, primer prevents subsequent coats of paint soaking back into the surface. Remember to choose the correct primer for each of the surfaces you are sealing.

However, before painting new or bare wood, a shellac solution, or knotter, must be painted on bare knots to seal them. This is called knotting, and prevents sap from bleeding through and discolouring later coats of paint.

TOOLS: 37mm (1½ in) paintbrush, scraper, hot-air gun, small brush for knotter

MATERIALS: Wire wool, metal primer, sandpaper, white spirit, clean cloth, knotter, wood primer

PRIMING METAL

1 Lightly rub down copper pipes with a pad of fine wire wool. This cleans off any grime and provides a key for the paint. This method can also be used if the pipes are to remain unpainted for an attractive polished finish.

2 Although it is not essential to prime copper piping, a coat of metal primer on pipes that become heated, such as central-heating radiator feeds, will help to prevent the top coat of paint from discolouring.

3 The most common ferrous-metal object in the home is a central-heating radiator. As it is a surface that gets hot, it must be painted when cold and primed with an oil-based metal primer. First, sand the corroded areas back to shiny metal. Wipe off any dust with a clean cloth and prime immediately before any oxidisation can occur.

KNOTTING AND PRIMING PREVIOUSLY PAINTED WOOD

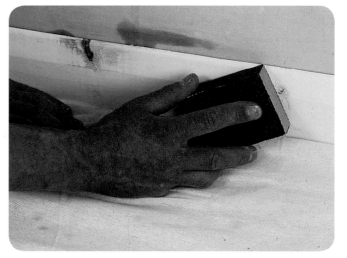

1 When treating an old bleeding knot which has discoloured the paintwork, remove the excess resin with a scraper. If the knot appears to be still active, carefully heat it with a hot-air gun, letting all the resin bubble out. Continue to scrape the area clean until no more bleeding occurs. When using a hot-air gun, follow all the precautions laid out on pages 40–41.

2 Once the knot is completely free of resin, smooth the area of wood around it with sandpaper wrapped round a sanding block. When the wood is quite smooth, take a clean cloth, moisten it with white spirit and wipe down the wood. This helps to pick up any remaining particles of wood dust or dirt, and cleans the prepared surface so that it is ready for painting.

PRIMING BARE WOOD

3 Apply the knotting solution sparingly, slightly overlapping it on to the surrounding wood. Two coats are normally required for a good seal. Always allow the first to dry thoroughly before adding the second. Then patch-prime the knot area.

Work the primer along and into the grain of the wood. As primer is quite thin, apply it sparingly, otherwise runs may occur. On bare wood, make sure every area is covered, but on previously painted wood, only the bare patches need priming.

Filling ceilings and walls

Cracks and holes in plasterwork are extremely common. They are caused either by slight movement in the building structure or just everyday wear and tear. To repair these defects, there are a number of different fillers available. Flexible fillers are best used in areas of potentially high movement, such as in cracks around door architraves. Pre-mixed and fine surface fillers come ready to use in a tub. However, powder filler is by far the most common type used. It is mixed with water, as and when it is needed.

TOOLS: Dusting brush, filling knife, 25mm (1in) paintbrush, caulking blade, sanding block, hammer

MATERIALS: Powder filler, water, fine-grade sandpaper, newspaper, batten, nails

1 Use the edge of a clean filling knife or scraper to rake out and clean up the damaged area. Brush out any loose debris with a dusting brush.

2 Pour the amount of powder filler required on to a clean board. An old paint tub lid is ideal for this purpose. When estimating how much you should mix up at a time, bear in mind that the filler will remain workable for approximately one hour. Gradually add water, mixing the filler into a creamy yet firm consistency.

3 Dampen the hole and the area around it with water. This lengthens the drying time so the filler is less likely to shrink. It also helps the filler and the plaster to bond.

IDEAL TOOL

When faced with an old wall that has many small cracks, a caulking blade helps to cover a large surface area very quickly. Use it in the same manner as a filling knife. It is also excellent for wide holes as its large blade can rest on the edges of the hole, keeping the filler level.

4 Load some filler on to the filling knife and draw it across the hole, using the flexibility of the knife to press the filler firmly into the hole. You may need to draw the filling knife across the hole two or three times to ensure that the area has been covered completely and that the filler is firmly in place. Always try to fill the hole slightly 'proud' of the surrounding area, to allow for small amounts of shrinkage. When the hole is filled, use the filling knife to clean off any excess filler from the wall around the hole to avoid any extra sanding when the filler has dried.

5 Sand the area when dry with a fine grade of sandpaper. Then run your fingers over the hole to check that it feels smooth and flush with the rest of the wall. If it is not, dust it off, wet as before and use a thin skim of filler to make good any indentations. With particularly deep holes, trying to fill them with just one load of filler can be difficult. Bulging will occur where the filler is unable to bond with the surrounding area. In this case, it may be necessary to use several thin coats to gradually build up the filler until it is level with the surrounding wall.

FILLING DEEP CRACKS

Sometimes it is necessary to fill a large, deep crack, perhaps in the corner of a room. Prior to filling, screw up a length of newspaper and, using a filling knife, press it very firmly into the crack. This will give the filler a base to sit on while it dries.

FILLING A CORNER

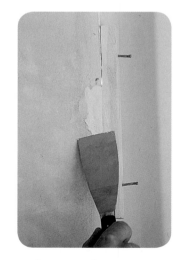

To repair an external corner, fix a length of wooden batten flush to one edge of the corner securing it in place with two nails. Fill the hole using a filling knife or caulking blade. When the filler has dried, sand the area, remove the batten and repeat the process on the adjacent corner edge. Finally, fill the four nail holes made by tacking on the batten. This technique will reproduce the original square corner edge.

Stripping wood

Modern paints have dramatically reduced the need to strip woodwork before they are reapplied. However, it is sometimes still necessary to strip off all previous layers of paint. For example, paint build-up can obscure fine detail or make doors and windows stick. Stripping is also essential before applying a natural wood finish.

There are two methods of stripping woodwork: by applying chemicals or using a hot-air gun. With chemical stripping, protective gloves and goggles are a sensible precaution, and it is wise to cover the surrounding area with dust sheets as stripping is often a very messy process. Ideally, doors should be taken off their hinges and laid flat on a work bench or trestles, so that you have easy access to all areas.

TOOLS: Gloves, goggles, old paintbrush, scraper, shavehook, hot-air gun, heat shield, electric sander, stiff brush

MATERIALS: Chemical stripper, white vinegar, clean cloth, sandpaper, white spirit, wire wool

USING A HOT-AIR GUN

When using a hot-air gun, take care not to point it at one area for too long as the heat will scorch the wood. Keep the gun moving slowly, only dwelling in one place long enough for the paint to begin bubbling. It is then ready to be scraped off.

STRIPPING CLOSE TO GLASS

Take great care when stripping areas that are close to glass such as a window frame. Most hot-air guns have heat shields which may be attached to the nozzle of the gun in order to deflect the heat and protect the glass from cracking.

IDEAL TOOL

A straight-sided shavehook is an ideal stripping tool as its pointed corners can be used to remove paint from the most intricate areas, such as the corners of door panels.

A combination shavehook, which has a blade with convex and concave edges, is useful for

removing paint from rounded or moulded surfaces.

CHEMICAL STRIPPING

1 Chemical strippers are available in liquid, gel, or paste forms so it is important to read the manufacturer's guidelines before use. The more liquid varieties should be applied in a dabbing motion using an old paintbrush. Do not brush out the stripper as it needs to be concentrated and densely applied in order to properly react with the paint. Wear protective gloves and apply paint strippers with care as they irritate the skin.

2 Leave the area for between ten minutes and half an hour to allow the stripper to break down the paint. Scrape away the bubbling debris using a shavehook. If all the paint does not come away at one time, further applications of stripper may be needed.

3 Once a surface is totally stripped, wash away any chemical remnants with clean water, or depending on the type of stripper used, clean down with white vinegar to neutralise the chemicals. Allow to dry and sand the wood thoroughly to produce a smooth, clean surface. An electric sander is ideal for large flat surfaces; always sand with the grain of the wood.

4 Finally, remove any dust from the surface by wiping down with a lint-free cloth dampened with some white spirit.

REMOVING INGRAINED PAINT

Paint that is lodged in the grain of wood can be removed by applying a small amount of chemical stripper to the area and rubbing the traces of paint away with some wire wool.

Filling wood

When preparing wood that is to be painted over, the types of filler used for walls and ceilings are also suitable to fill cracks or holes in wood. However, if the wood is to be stained or varnished, a stainable filler must be used so that it can be coloured to match and blend in with the surrounding wood.

Powder and ready-mixed fillers are ideal for dealing with chips in paintwork or nail holes. However, for areas that might experience some slight movement, such as cracked door panels and architraves, flexible fillers are more suitable as they will tolerate slight movement.

TOOLS: Hammer, nail punch, filling knife, filler board, scraper, dusting brush, skeleton gun/filler dispenser

MATERIALS: Sandpaper, powder filler, flexible filler

POWDER FILLER

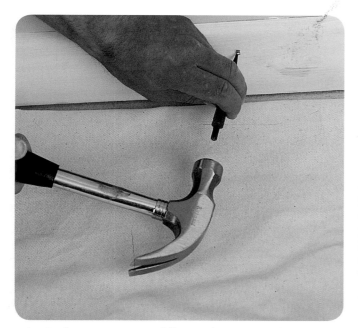

1 Before starting to fill wood areas, such as a skirting board, always check for any protruding nails. They will spoil the overall finish and may cause an injury when the wood is sanded. Use a nail punch and hammer to drive nails into and just below the surface of the wood.

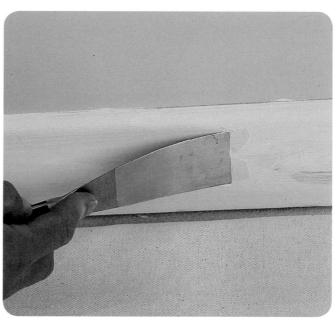

2 Fill the hole slightly proud using a filling knife. Then wet the blade of the knife and draw it across the filled area, smoothing the filler to help reduce the amount of sanding needed. When the filler has dried, sand the wood back to a smooth finish.

FLEXIBLE FILLER

1 When filling a cracked joint, rake out any loose paint or dust using the sharp edge of a scraper. Sand the area smooth and use a dusting brush to clear away the debris.

2 Cut the nozzle of the filler tube to the size required. Gently pull the dispenser trigger while drawing the end of the nozzle down the crack, squeezing the filler into the gap.

3 Run a wetted finger over the filler, pushing it into the recess and creating a smooth finish. It is important to smooth the filler soon after it is applied as it dries out very quickly.

3 If bubbles and flaking on an old painted surface are extensive, you may need to strip off all the paint back to the bare wood (see pages 40–41). However, in a small area, simply shave off all the loose material using a scraper, taking care not to dig into the wood itself.

4 Sand down the area with a medium-grade sandpaper or block. Then use a fine-grade paper to feather the edges of the bare wood with the surrounding painted area. If the indentation is still noticeable, skim with a thin layer of filler and sand to a smooth finish when dry.

Cleaning down and sealing

Both these processes are vital in order to stabilise wall surfaces before any sort of decoration takes place. Either painting or papering over unstable or dirty areas may look acceptable at first, but the finish will inevitably deteriorate before long.

Although these all-important initial steps cannot be seen when the decorating is completed, they are absolutely essential for a good-quality and long-lasting finish.

TOOLS: Bucket, stirring stick, gloves, sponge, 37, 100 and 125mm (1½, 4 and 5in) paintbrushes

MATERIALS: PVA adhesive, emulsion paint, damp sealant or oil-based undercoat, aerosol stain block, sugar soap, water

CLEANING DOWN

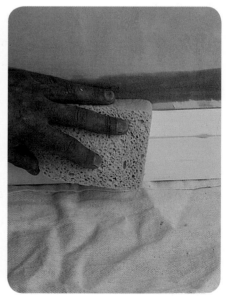

1 Ceilings, walls and woodwork should be cleaned down using a solution of sugar soap or mild detergent. Mix with warm water as per the manufacturer's instructions.

2 Wear protective gloves when using sugar soap as it irritates the skin. Make sure you clean all surfaces thoroughly, removing any dust and impurities.

3 The sugar soap solution must be rinsed off every surface, using plenty of clear water and a sponge. Once it is quite clean, allow the surface to dry completely before continuing to decorate.

SEALING

1 Once all surfaces have been prepared and cleaned down, PVA adhesive is ideal for sealing all porous or dusty surfaces. Primers can also be used, but on large areas they will take longer to apply and tend to be less economic. A coat of PVA solution provides both a sound surface for painting or acts as a 'size' if you are going to use lining paper. Read the manufacturer's guidelines for mixing, but as a rule 1 part PVA to 5 parts water is the standard dilution required.

2 Apply the PVA solution liberally, making sure of good coverage. 'Pick up' and brush in any drips or runs that may occur. When dry, run your hand over the surface to check whether it is still dusty or powdery. If so, add a second coat.

3 New plaster surfaces can also be primed or sealed in a number of ways. Water-based products are the easiest option. If you are going to paint directly on top of the plaster, diluted white emulsion is ideal for two reasons. First, because emulsion is permeable, any remaining moisture in the plaster can dry through the emulsion. Second, this will give a more uniform wall colour and will save having to apply more coats of paint than is absolutely necessary. Again, ensure good coverage when applying. (See Using a Brush, pages 74–75, if you have any problems.)

COVERING DAMP STAINS

Damp stains are common, but can be cured with the correct treatment. Consult a professional if a damp patch is clearly active as you may have an exterior problem that needs attention. If the stain is old and dry, or the problem has been cured, apply a proprietary damp sealant or an oil-based undercoat over the area.

Some nondescript stains keep persisting through paintwork. Proprietary aerosol stain blocks will generally take care of marks that are the most difficult to cover.

LINING

Whether you are eventually going to paint or wallpaper a room, using lining paper on walls and ceilings makes all the difference for a professional rather than an amateur finish. Although the use of lining paper is often considered unnecessary by many enthusiasts, it does give a flatter, more even surface, smoothing out imperfections and giving an ideal surface on which to decorate.

There is a commonly held belief that you must line horizontally before wallpapering, and vertically for painting purposes. The choice is a purely practical one, however: the aim is to cover the ceiling and/or walls with the fewest number of lengths, to make best use of time and effort.

This section shows you how to approach lining a room using the correct techniques, and how to overcome any problems that you may encounter.

Preparation

Before starting to hang any lining paper, decide how many rolls are needed to complete the job. Using a tape measure and the table to the right, you can be surprisingly accurate.

The diagram on page 93 illustrates the best way to calculate surface areas. There is no right or wrong place to start, as each surface should be treated as separate to the next. Mentally divide your room into different areas (see below right) and decide on the most practical direction to line; this will help you decide your order of work. Begin with the ceiling as it is, in fact, easier than most walls because there are fewer obstacles to work around.

When lining a wall horizontally, start at the top and work down, as working from the bottom up may cause problems when joining the paper at higher levels, especially after papering around obstacles such as doors or windows.

TOOLS: and paper, 2 buckets, measuring jug, stirring stick

MATERIALS: Packet of wallpaper paste, water

2 When mixing up paste ensure all the equipment is clean. Always read the manufacturer's instructions as they can vary between different brands of paste. Measure out the correct quantity of cold water using a measuring jug.

1 When setting out equipment it is important to be well organised. Place buckets of paste and clean water under the table to save space and to avoid accidents. Always keep your table clean and clear of obstacles. Try to keep everything to hand to save time and energy.

3 Start to stir the water, then sprinkle the powder slowly into the bucket. Continue to stir for 2 minutes after adding all the paste. Leave it to stand for another 3 minutes, then stir again to ensure there are no lumps. It is now ready to use.

USING A PLATFORM

Working on a safe, solid platform is very important, especially when papering a ceiling. Trestles are excellent supports, but two step-ladders with a sturdy plank are a good compromise. Remember to have extra support underneath the middle of the plank when covering a large area.

MEASURING UP

Follow steps 1 and 2 on page 93, and calculate the amount of lining paper needed from the table below. There is no need to add on any extra for pattern repeat when using lining paper.

ROLLS OF LINING PAPER NEEDED			
Total Surface Area to Line		No of rolls	
sq m	sq yd		
5	6	1	For every additional
10	12	2	5sq m (6sq yd), add
15	18	3	one roll of lining
			paper.

Standard roll of lining paper is 56cm x 10.05m = 5.628sq m (22in x 11yd = 6¾sq yd). The excess of 0.628sq m (¾sq yd) per roll allows for both trimming and wastage.

If you are not using standard rolls, simply work out the surface area of the rolls you are using and create your own table by the same method as above.

ORDER OF WORK

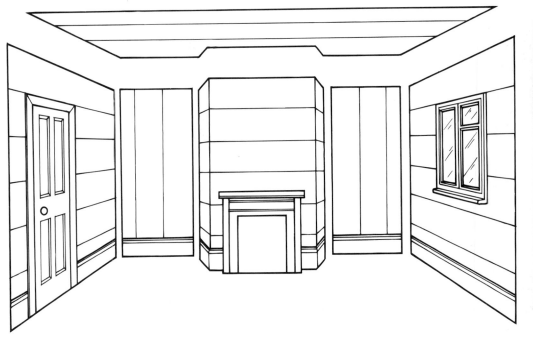

DOUBLE LINING

On particularly uneven walls, the final finish may look better if you apply two layers of lining paper before the top wallpaper. Ensure that the joins on the second layer do not coincide with the seams of the first.

Cutting and pasting

When cutting lengths of lining paper always add 10cm (4in) to your basic measurement to allow a 5cm (2in) overlap at each end for final trimming.

After pasting, allow time for the paste to soak into the paper, as this makes it more pliable and easier to work with.

Soaking times vary, so always check the manufacturer's guidelines. Write a number on each length as you work. This helps keep them in the right order if you have more than one length soaking at a time.

TOOLS: Pasting table, tape measure, pencil, steel rule, scissors, pasting brush, paper-hanging brush, sponge

MATERIALS: Lining paper, bucket of wallpaper paste, water

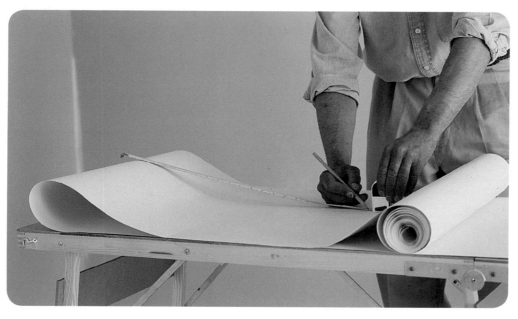

1 Carefully unroll the lining paper along the length of the pasting table. If long pieces of paper are going to be needed, gently fold the paper back on itself along the table. Use a tape measure to work out the length of paper required. Make a pencil mark in the centre of the paper where the first piece is to be cut.

2 Keep the edges of the length of paper flush with the edges of the table. This will help to ensure a square cut. Place a straight edge at the pencil mark, check it is square and draw a line along its length.

3 Cut a neat, straight line along the pencil line. Then lie the paper flat along the table with the excess paper falling over one end. Use the paper-hanging brush to hold the other end of the paper still.

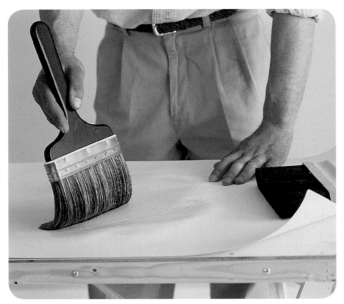

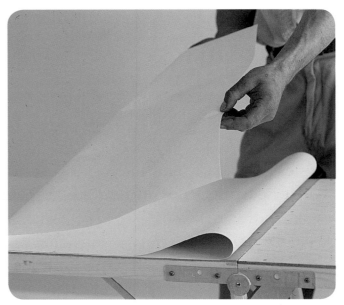

4 Line up the paper flush with the edges of the table, to avoid getting paste on the face of the paper. Apply the paste evenly, working from the centre outwards, ensuring the whole area is covered.

5 Once the paper on the table is pasted, gently fold the pasted end over, starting a concertina. Pull this along to one end of the table, again with the paper-hanging brush anchoring the other end.

6 Paste the remaining paper, working up to the end of the table. Always make sure that the paste is applied evenly, and that all areas of the paper are covered with paste. Remove any excess paste from the right side of the paper with a damp sponge, as it may stain if it is allowed to dry.

7 Keep folding the paper back on itself to make up a finished concertina, taking care that the paper does not crease. Remove the completed concertina from the table and leave it to soak for the required time. Wipe the table down with a slightly damp sponge to clean up any excess paste.

Ceilings

Always try to line across the longest dimension of the room as fewer lengths will be required, and this will save time.

Make sure that you have a solid platform from which to work. Trestles and planks are ideal as they enable you to get close to the wall–ceiling junction at both ends of the platform. Adjust its height so that the top of your head is 25–30cm (10–12in) from the ceiling.

Lining the ceiling is not as difficult as it may appear. Once the first length is hung and a straight edge established, subsequent lengths become easier and less time consuming.

TOOLS: Trestles and plank, paper-hanging brush, pencil, scissors, small brush for pasting edges, sponge

MATERIALS: Lining paper, bucket of wallpaper paste, water

1 Arrange the trestles and plank under the area where you wish to start. Carefully lay out the concertina along the plank. Pick up one end of the paper.

2 Start papering at the edge of the ceiling. Take care to keep the paper edge parallel with the length of the adjacent wall. Using the paper-hanging brush push the paper into the junction, allowing for 5cm (2in) overlap.

3 When the paper is held securely at one end, move slowly along the plank, brushing the paper from the centre out in a herringbone fashion. Keep the edge of the paper tight to the wall using it as a guide. Brush the length into position and repeat step 2 at the opposite end.

4 When the length is hung, run a pencil along where the wall and ceiling meet to make a straight line. Alternatively, run a pair of scissors along to make a crease.

EASIER CEILINGS
Papering a ceiling is easier and less tiring with two people. One can hold the paper while the other manoeuvres it into place.

5 Carefully peel back the paper. Using the paper-hanging scissors, cut a neat, straight edge along the pencil guideline or scissor crease.

6 Push the paper back into position. Work along the length, checking for bubbles or lifting at the edge. Apply extra paste to edges where needed.

7 After each length is hung, immediately wipe off any surplus paste from all the surfaces, or it will stain them.

Hang the next length in the same way as the first but place the edge of the new length a little way from that of the first. Slide the paper into position making a neat butt join.

Walk down the plank brushing out the paper, making sure you keep the two edges of the join completely flush. Trim off at each end as before.

DEALING WITH GAPS
If the wall is not square, you will find that a gap appears along the wall–ceiling junction as you work along the length of the ceiling. A small gap of 5mm or less can be filled (see page 59), but if a larger gap appears, simply move the paper closer to the wall, allowing an overlap on to the wall. This overlap can be trimmed using the technique shown in steps 4–6 above.

Ceiling roses

Most ceilings have at least one light fitting and by far the most common is the ceiling rose. Two methods can be used to paper around them. The first, shown in steps 1–5, is to pull the pendant through a cut in the paper. The second and more reliable method, shown in the box on page 55, is to measure the distance between the starting wall and the ceiling rose to ensure that a seam between lengths will coincide with the pendant.

TOOLS: Trestles and plank, paper-hanging brush, scissors, craft knife, small brush for pasting edges, sponge, screwdriver

MATERIALS: Lining paper, bucket of wallpaper paste, water, clean cloth

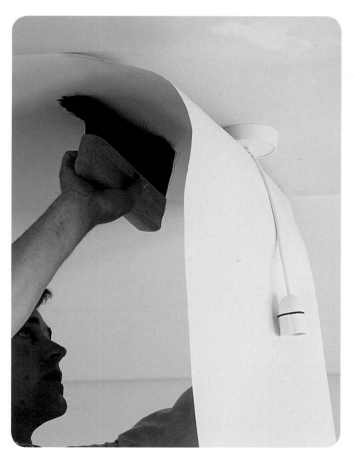

ELECTRICAL SAFETY
Always remember to turn off the power supply before undertaking any work around electrical fittings.

1 When you reach the ceiling rose with a length of pasted paper, gently brush the paper over the pendant, so that you can see where the rose is located in relation to the paper.

2 Support the unfixed side of the paper with one hand. Using scissors, carefully mark the location of the centre of the rose on the underside of the paper. Make a small cut.

3 Gently pull the pendant through the cut, taking care not to tear the paper. Then brush the remaining length of paper away, continuing on to the wall on the other side of the room.

4 Using the scissors, make a series of small cuts out to the edge of the rose. Work right round the rose, but do not cut any further than the edge of the plastic circle itself.

5 Crease around the edge of the rose and trim with a craft knife. Brush out any remaining bubbles from the entire length, and wipe off any excess paste from the pendant with a dry cloth.

SEAM JOIN

1 Turn off the power supply. Unscrew the rose's casing by hand and loosen off the retaining screws. Then allow the entire pendant to drop approximately 5cm (2in).

2 Using the paper-hanging brush, tuck in the paper edges underneath the rose. Tighten the screws and screw the ceiling rose casing back into position.

Walls

Lining paper on walls can be hung either horizontally or vertically. The choice is purely a practical one. Vertical lining is ideal for small alcoves as fewer lengths are required, whereas a long wall can be quickly covered with horizontal lengths. Vertical lining uses a vertical corner of the wall as a straight edge, whereas horizontal lining takes its guide from where the wall and the ceiling meet.

As horizontal lengths are normally longer than vertical lengths, a much larger concertina is required. To overcome this problem, make the folds smaller so that the concertina is more compact and easier to manage with one hand.

TOOLS: Trestles and plank, paper-hanging brush, pencil, scissors, craft knife, small brush for pasting edges, sponge

MATERIALS: Lining paper, bucket of wallpaper paste, water

HORIZONTAL LINING

1 Start papering at the top of the wall leaving a 5cm (2in) overlap around the corner onto the next area of wall. Line up the top edge of the paper with the wall and ceiling junction. If the wall–ceiling junction is not square, move the paper to overlap onto the ceiling and trim as usual when the remainder of the length is hung.

2 Slowly release the folds of the concertina, smoothing the paper along the wall using a paper-hanging brush. Brushing from the centre of the paper outwards, continue along to the other corner, keeping the top edge of the paper flush with the wall–ceiling junction.

3 Mark a line at the corner with a pencil, or crease the corner with scissors, then gently pull the paper away from the wall. Trim with the scissors or a craft knife.

4 Push the paper back into the corner with the brush. Extra paste may be needed if the edge of the paper has dried out during trimming. Repeat steps 3 and 4 at the other end of the length.

CROOKED ROOMS

If the wall or ceiling is very crooked (and it has been necessary to overlap paper on to the ceiling) you will be unable to use the wall–ceiling junction as a guideline to hang the entire length. So that you do not find yourself papering this first length at a sharp angle, it is wise to hold a spirit level at the bottom edge to ensure that the first length is hung straight. When lining vertically, a spirit level can also be used as a guideline when unsquare walls are causing problems.

VERTICAL LINING

1 Vertical lining is an excellent way to deal with problem areas such as pipes. Start the first length flush with the pipes and push the paper behind them so the join will be hidden.

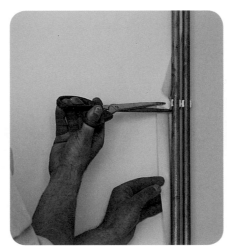

2 Mark the location of the pipe clips with a pencil and make two small cuts to the edge of the clips. Push the paper around the clips and trim off the excess paper.

3 Cut another length and butt-join it to the previously hung paper. Smooth and trim as before. Wipe any excess paste off the pipes as it will otherwise react with paint, if used.

Corners

When lining, the only corners you need to paper around are external (that is, those that stick out). At internal corners it is better to begin or end paper, because trying to bend it around the corner usually causes bubbles and problems with adhesion. Using filler on internal corners, as shown here, is a far wiser and ultimately neater option. If you have difficulty with an external corner that is uneven or not square, a manufactured butt join is the ideal solution.

TOOLS: Trestles and plank, paper-hanging brush, scissors, steel rule, craft knife, sponge

MATERIALS: Lining paper, bucket of wallpaper paste, water, flexible filler, powder filler, sandpaper, cloth

EXTERNAL CORNERS

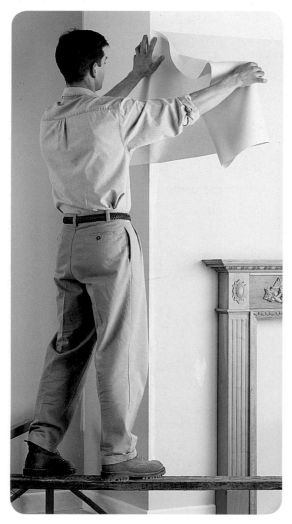

1 Approach the external corner holding the horizontal concertina in one hand. Use the other hand to push the paper up to the corner edge, keeping the horizontal edge of the length of paper flush with the edge of the ceiling or the paper above, forming a neat butt join.

2 Fold the paper around the corner using the paper-hanging brush to expel any bubbles. Make sure that the top edge of the paper is not overlapping the paper already hung above it.

3 Run your fingers gently down the corner to check for any wrinkles or creases. Smooth them out, if necessary. Once the corner is neat and problem-free, proceed along the the wall with the rest of the length.

UNEVEN EXTERNAL CORNERS

1 For an uneven corner, bend the horizontal length around the corner and trim off all except a 5cm (2in) overlap. Do this with each (horizontal) length on the corner. Hang the next length (on the next section of wall) vertically, on top of the overlaps.

2 On the wall with the vertical length, place a straight edge 3cm (1¼in) from the corner. Using a craft knife, cut a straight line down the straight edge. Then move the straight edge and repeat the process, so continuing the cut from ceiling to skirting.

3 Pull back the paper and gently remove the excess (overlapping) strips of paper. Push the paper back into position using the paper-hanging brush. Finally, wipe the area with a damp sponge to remove any excess paste.

INTERNAL CORNERS

1 Because we recommend trimming all lengths at an internal corner, for a perfect finish, run a bead of flexible filler along all internal corners, and along the skirting board top.

2 Smooth along the filler with a wetted finger. This will neaten the finish, and prevent the edges of the paper from lifting later. Wipe off any excess filler with a clean, damp cloth.

FILLING GAPS

Small gaps between lengths are sometimes unavoidable. These can be overcome using a fine surface filler, and then sanded smooth.

Doors and obstacles

Some room features – such as door surrounds, flush windows and fireplaces – protrude out from the wall, and lining paper must be cut to fit around them. No matter what the obstacle, the technique used is much the same. A neat and exact finish is produced by precisely trimming into angles and along edges. The examples shown here include a fireplace that needs complex trimming, and a door because, quite simply, every room has one.

TOOLS: Trestles and plank, paper-hanging brush, pencil, scissors, craft knife, small brush for pasting edges, sponge

MATERIALS: Lining paper, bucket of wallpaper paste, water

FIREPLACES

1 When the paper reaches the fireplace, allow it to flap over the top corner of the mantlepiece. Make a cut diagonally towards the upper part of the corner, taking care that the paper below the cut does not tear under its own weight.

2 Having made this initial cut, ignore the paper fold on top of the fireplace for the time being. With the aid of the paper-hanging brush and scissors, push the paper gently into the angles of the mantlepiece making small right-angled cuts to allow it to lie flat on the wall.

3 Trim the small flaps with a craft knife, taking care to get as close as possible to the moulding, and without leaving any gaps. Continue to paper along the top of the mantlepiece and repeat steps 1–3 at the other corner. Then trim the fold on top of the mantlepiece.

4 It is vital to clean the excess paste off ornate obstacles immediately in order to prevent later staining or discoloration. Use a clean dampened sponge, and pay particular attention to paste that may have found its way into intricate details.

DOORS

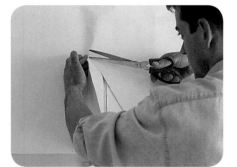

2 Both hands now freed, feel for the corner of the architrave. Cut diagonally towards this point with scissors. Carefully draw back the excess paper hanging over the door. Using the paper-hanging brush, firmly push the paper covering the wall above the door into the edge of the architrave. Do the same with the other corner of the architrave.

3 Using a craft knife, trim away the excess paper, working carefully around the side and top edges of the door architrave.

1 Allow the length of paper to fall over the corner of the door architrave. Continue to hang the length along the rest of the wall, loosely attaching it to the wall surface.

Recessed windows

The technique for lining around a recessed window combines a number of steps already covered in this chapter. However, the order in which you hang the various lengths of paper is vital to produce the best possible finish. The particular method shown here will also come in useful when tackling similar types of shapes and obstacles, such as recessed doors or alcoves.

TOOLS: Trestles and plank, paper-hanging brush, scissors, craft knife, small brush for pasting edges, steel rule, sponge

MATERIALS: Lining paper, wallpaper paste, water

1 Hang the first length of paper horizontally, as usual, allowing the paper to span right across the recess. When you have made sure the paper is correctly butt-joined to the previous length, return to the window and make two vertical cuts approximately 1.5cm (⅝in) in from the corners of the recess. Carefully continue these cuts right up to the top edge of the window recess.

2 Starting in the middle, use the paper-hanging brush to push the flap of paper you have made back into the recess, expelling any air bubbles as you do so. Move the brush along the edge continuing the process until the paper is properly in place on the ceiling of the recess.

3 Make sure the paper has been firmly positioned in the junction between the window frame and the upper part of the recess, before trimming as usual.

4 Fold the 1.5cm (⅝in) flap around the corner of the vertical recess using your brush and fingers to expel any air bubbles if necessary. Add extra paste to the edge of the paper if it has dried out too quickly. Hang the next length, again allowing a flap of paper approximately 1.5cm (⅝in) wide to fold around into the recess. Repeat this process at the opposite side of the window recess.

5 Depending on the height of the window recess, you may need to hang further lengths of paper before finally reaching the window sill. At the sill, carefully trim the paper using a series of right-angled cuts, moulding the paper around the corner of the sill and underneath it. Once you have successfully dealt with one side, repeat this process when the paper reaches the opposite corner of the sill.

6 Measure and cut a panel of paper to finish off each vertical return of the recess. Line up the straight edge of the paper with the vertical corner, covering the trimmed overlaps of the previous lengths.

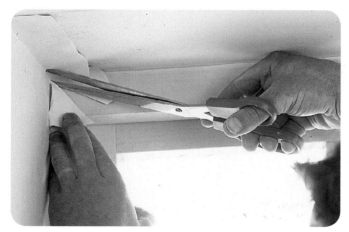

7 Make diagonal cuts into the top corner of the recess. Repeat this at the bottom corner, to assist final trimming. Any small gaps can be filled using the methods shown on page 59.

REFINING YOUR TECHNIQUE

You may find that this technique of overlapping different pieces of lining paper does not produce a completely flat surface, as the small cuts around the vertical, external corners of the recess may be visible in the finished result. Faced with this problem, there are two points to consider. First, it is likely that curtains will eventually cover these imperfections. Second, as you become more skilled, you may prefer to try the manufactured butt-join technique shown in Uneven External Corners (see page 59).

Electrical wall fittings

It goes without saying that light switches and electrical sockets are very common features on walls. It often appears to be difficult to paper around them neatly but if care is taken, they need not present a problem. It is important to make a neat job of light switches as every time you enter or leave a room, your eyes are naturally drawn towards them. Whatever their size or shape, the technique for coping with them remains the same.

Always remember to turn off the electricity at the mains or consumer unit before working near any electrical fitting.

TOOLS: Trestles and plank, paper-hanging brush, pencil, scissors, screwdriver, craft knife, small brush for pasting edges, sponge

MATERIALS: Lining paper, bucket of wallpaper paste, water, dry cloth

1 Turn off the electricity at the mains. Paper directly over the top of the power point or switch, butt-joining the paper, as usual.

2 Brush gently over the fixture, allowing it to form an impression in the paper. Take care not to tear the paper when carrying out this step.

3 Holding the paper firmly over the switch or power point, make a small diagonal pencil mark, 5mm (¼in) in from each of its corners.

4 Using scissors, carefully make four diagonal cuts from the centre of the switch out to the pencil marks.

5 Trim off each of the four flaps, just inside the outer edge of the switch, so that a small amount of overlap remains over the switch plate.

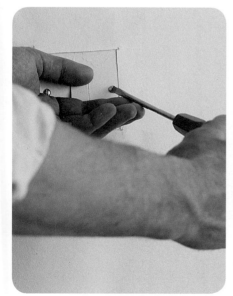

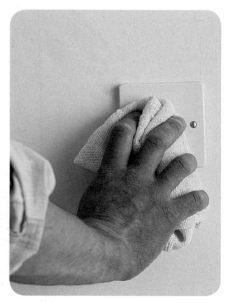

6 Unscrew the two retaining screws that hold the face plate on to the switch itself. It is not necessary to unscrew them completely, but just far enough to move the face plate a little way out from the wall.

7 Ease the face plate out from the wall, rotating it slightly from side to side. Be careful when pushing the face plate through the paper as erratic movements will tear it. Use the brush to push the paper behind the plate.

8 Wipe off any excess paste with a dry cloth. Put the face plate back and tighten up the screws, making sure the small paper flaps are firmly tucked behind the face plate. Take care not to over-tighten the screws.

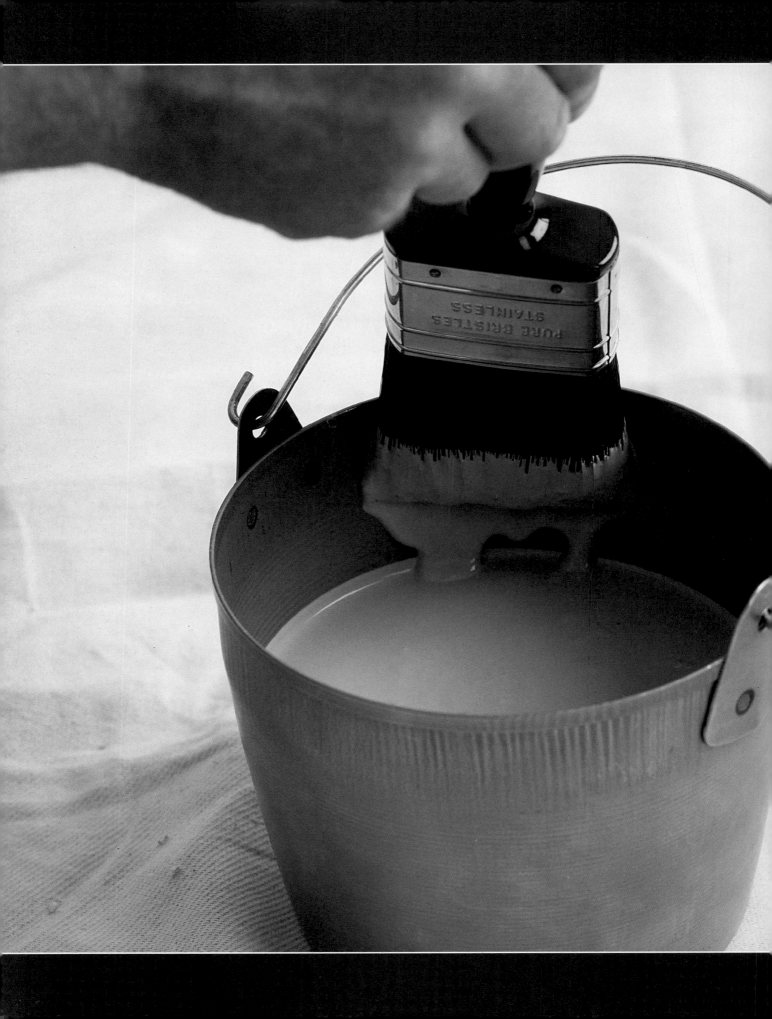

Painting

With all the 'dirty' work done – sanding, filling, priming and general preparation – the actual painting can be the most enjoyable part of redecorating your home. In this section, all the different techniques and methods for applying both undercoats and top coats to interior surfaces are illustrated. Always remember to read the manufacturer's guidelines on the number of coats required for a particular type of paint, and use the recommendations given on pages 28–29 to ensure that you use the correct order and system of application for whatever finish you have chosen. Allow adequate drying time between coats and never rush your work, as this will inevitably spoil the overall finish.

Preparation

The order in which you carry out your work is very important as it will ensure that you do each particular task once. There is nothing more frustrating than having to repaint something because of bad planning. As a basic rule when painting interiors, paint the ceiling first, followed by the walls and then the woodwork, and when painting exteriors, start at the top of the house and work down. Keeping to this order will make sure that any splashes will be covered by each subsequent stage of painting. Painting smaller items, such as window furniture, should be considered as finishing touches. Whether using solvent- or water-based paints, during every stage keep the doors and windows open in order to give adequate ventilation.

TOOLS: Dusting brush, lid opener, stirring stick, paint kettle, 2 buckets, dust sheet

MATERIALS: Paint, masking tape, kitchen foil, gauze cloth, large rubber band

PREPARING THE PAINT

1 Before opening the paint can, use a dusting brush to wipe the lid clean, as grit and dirt tend to collect around the rim. If you do not do this, debris may fall into the paint as you remove the lid.
Prise the lid open with a blunt instrument. A tool designed for this task can be bought cheaply and saves damaging expensive items such as screwdrivers or chisels.

2 Some paints, such as non-drip gloss and solid emulsion, must not be stirred before use, so always read the manufacturer's guidelines. Otherwise, most paints need a thorough stir. Use either a proprietary stirring stick or a piece of wooden dowel. As you stir, try to use a lifting motion. This brings up any sediment from the bottom of the can, and ensures that the pigments are mixed thoroughly.

3 It is advisable to decant the paint into a paint kettle for several reasons. First, the original paint can will stay cleaner for storage. Second, if the kettle is knocked over less paint is spilt. Third, carrying a heavy can up a ladder can throw you off balance. Finally, if any debris gets into the kettle it can be cleaned out and refilled from the original can. Lining a paint kettle with kitchen foil will save time when cleaning it out or using a different colour.

4 When using paint left over from a previous job, you may find a skin has formed. Remove this from the can before stirring. The paint may still have lumps, so it is advisable to sieve it before use. Place some stockinette or gauze cloth over the paint kettle and hold it in place with a large rubber band. Pour the paint slowly into the kettle. This technique can be used when you replace the paint to prevent any debris getting back into the main can.

NON-DRIP PAINTS

Solid emulsion and other non-drip paints have been created purely to make painting easier. They do not need stirring and they cause less mess during painting because of their special consistency.

THINNING PAINT

Water is usually used to thin water-based paints, white spirit for solvent-based – but always follow the manufacturer's instructions. To ensure accuracy with the thinning ratio, use two calibrated buckets. Stir the thinned paint to ensure a consistent solution.

Using a roller

Using a roller is the quickest and most efficient way of covering large surface areas. Rollers can be used to apply solvent-based paints, but they are most often used with water-based paints such as emulsion or acrylic eggshell. Roller heads have become more varied in recent years with a range of sizes and textures, making them practically indispensable to the modern decorator.

TOOLS: Roller, roller tray, textured roller, extension pole, roller shield, radiator roller

MATERIALS: Paint, clingfilm

1 A roller tray consists of two parts: the paint reservoir, and a ribbed slope to wipe off excess paint and allow it to run back into the reservoir. Pour the prepared paint into the tray's reservoir, filling it to just below the start of the slope.

2 Dip the roller head into the paint reservoir and run it firmly up and down the ribs of the slope to distribute the paint evenly round the roller. Take care not to overload the head or paint will drip and splatter everywhere.

3 Move the loaded roller over the wall surface using light, even strokes. Working the roller too fast will cause a fine mist of paint spray, and should be avoided. Each time the roller is reloaded, apply it to an unpainted surface and then work back to the previously painted area in a series of overlapping strokes.

SPECIAL ROLLERS AND TOOLS

Extension poles

These are attached to the roller handle and are effective when painting ceilings and stairwells. They can also be useful when painting low areas. However, roller extensions should not be used when painting up a ladder as you need two hands to operate them properly.

Textured rollers

Textured paints are similar to very thick emulsion and are excellent for covering up small cracks. Here a textured roller is used to create a stippled effect. The paint tends to dry quickly, so it is advisable to work in small areas of approximately 1sq m (1sq yd) at a time.

Roller shield

A roller with a plastic shield is a useful tool, especially when painting a ceiling. It helps avoid both roller spray and dripping from the edges of the roller frame. It can be added to an extension pole for painting ceilings, but check that it matches your pole before buying it.

4 Work around and behind awkward areas such as pipes and radiators with a long-handled radiator roller. Without this special tool, these areas might otherwise be difficult to reach.

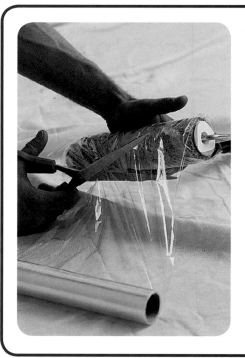

TEMPORARY STORAGE

When you have to pause during painting – between coats, for example – wrap a short length of clingfilm around the roller head, making sure to expel any trapped air. This saves having to wash out and dry the roller at frequent intervals.

Pads and sprayers

Paint pads, sprayers and spray guns are alternatives to the more traditional rollers and brushes.

Paint pads make less spray and mess than rollers. Their design has been improved in recent years, so now they can be used successfully, not just for covering large flat surfaces, but also for small, intricate areas such as window beads and door architraves.

Airless spray guns have also become more efficient and, on the whole, have dropped dramatically in price, making them a possibility for the home decorator. The technique for spraying can be mastered surprisingly quickly and can give a very satisfying and professional finish.

TOOLS: Paint pads, paint tray, paint sprayer, goggles, respirator mask, gloves, dust sheets

MATERIALS: Masking tape, paint

PAINT PADS

1 Paint pads are flat and rectangular with closely packed, short, fine fibres. They produce a smooth paint finish when used carefully. Pads come in a range of sizes for all-round use.

2 When loading a paint pad, gently dip the fibres into the tray reservoir. Take care not to immerse the pad head, as this will cause drips when it is used on the wall. Pull the pad over the ribbed slope to distribute the paint evenly. Some trays come with a built-in ribbed roller to remove the excess paint.

3 To paint the wall, use light even strokes in all directions, slightly overlapping each stroke. Pads need reloading more often than rollers as their fibres cannot hold as much paint. Paint pads tend to be faster than a brush but slower than a roller. There may be a need for extra coats as although pads apply paint very evenly, they tend to produce thinner coats. Extension poles can be attached to paint-pad heads to reach awkward areas such as ceilings.

PAINT SPRAYERS

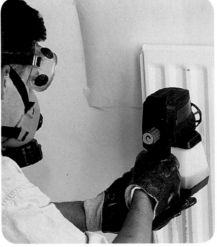

1 Mask up all the surrounding areas that are not to be painted. Thin the paint if necessary, following the manufacturer's guidelines, and pour into the reservoir of the spray gun. Attach the reservoir to the gun and select the correct nozzle for the type of paint and finish required.

2 It is wise to test the spray gun and your spraying technique on some old newspaper before starting the particular job in hand. As the paint spray may spatter slightly when the gun is started, first spray slightly away from the area that is to be painted, and then slowly sweep across the actual area.

3 As you progress, use a steady deliberate motion, slightly overlapping the paint that has been already applied. Never be tempted to return to a patchy area: the paint may run because too much has been applied in one coat. Many thin coats are definitely preferable to one or two thick ones.

SPRAYING TECHNIQUE

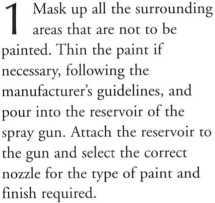

This shows the ideal progression of the spray gun across the surface to be painted. Work past the end of the completed area before stopping.

Keep the nozzle about 30cm (12in) away from the surface at all times, and spray parallel to the surface.

SPRAY GUNS

An airless spray gun is electrically operated and relies on paint being pumped, under high pressure, from a large reservoir or hopper up a tube to the gun and then on to the wall surface. Compressed-air sprayers feed air from a compressor up a tube into a small reservoir of paint, positioned directly below the gun. The paint is then mixed with the air and sprayed on the wall by pulling the gun's trigger.

Using a brush

Brushes have long been the most popular and adaptable tools for painting nearly all surfaces. A brush has been designed to cope with almost every problem, from large areas to seemingly unreachable gaps behind radiators. Pure bristle brushes are still the professional choice, although synthetic alternatives are available. Brush prices vary considerably, but it is worth paying a little extra for quality. Cheaper options tend to be stiffer with shorter bristles, and moult continually, making a good finish hard to achieve.

TOOLS: Paintbrushes, paint kettle, paint shield

MATERIALS: Paint, lint-free cloth

1 Before starting to paint, flick the end of the brush and wipe it on a lint-free cloth to remove any loose bristles and dust. New brushes should be used to prime or undercoat wood to get rid of bristles which are often loosened when they are first used. Such brushes can then be used for top coats at a later date.

2 Dip the brush into the paint so that about one-third of the bristles are immersed. Raise the brush and gently push the bristles against the side of the paint kettle to get rid of excess paint. Avoid scraping the brush on the edge of the kettle as this will build up paint on the inside and form drips down the outside.

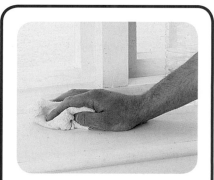

FINAL CLEANING
Even after thorough preparation and cleaning down of surfaces to be painted, dust can still accumulate on horizontal areas such as window sills. Just before painting, wipe them with a lint-free cloth dampened with a little white spirit. They will dry quickly by evaporation, leaving completely dust-free surfaces on which an excellent finish can be achieved.

3 When using water-based paint on a large area such as a wall, choose a 100–125mm (4–5in) paintbrush, as one that is any larger will be heavy and will quickly tire your arm. Apply the paint to the wall with short, overlapping horizontal and vertical strokes. Work in areas of approximately 1sq m (1sq yd) at a time.

4 With the brush unloaded, remove any visible brush marks by lightly drawing the bristles across the painted surface, again using a series of horizontal and vertical strokes. This technique is known as 'laying off'. Having completed this process, move on to the adjoining area, always working away from the wet edge.

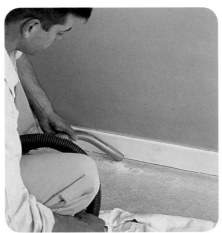

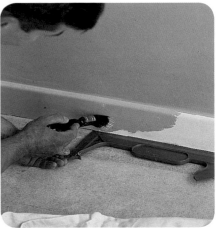

5 When applying solvent-based paint to a large area, make three vertical, parallel strips of about 30cm (12in) long. Without reloading the brush, blend the strips together horizontally, brushing out the paint. To complete the laying-off process finish with light vertical strokes.

6 Always try to keep the decorating area as clean and dust free as possible. A vacuum cleaner is the most efficient way of keeping the room clean, and is especially useful at skirting-board level. If any dirt or grit is picked up on the skirting board, sand it lightly between coats.

7 When painting the skirting board, place a paint shield or a clean piece of cardboard against the bottom, parallel to the floorboards or carpet. This will ensure that no dirt is picked up from the floor by the brush and transfered to the painted surface. It will also protect the flooring.

Cutting in

Although rollers and paint pads are efficient for covering large areas such as walls and ceilings, it is still necessary to finish the job off around the edges. This is known as 'cutting in' or beading.

When using a roller, for example, you can cut in either before or after doing the rollering, as long as the paint edges are still wet when either process is carried out. This is because wet and dry paint edges, on the same coat, can cause an unsightly framing effect. When drying conditions are quick (normally with all water-based paints), take each ceiling or wall at a time, completing it before going on to the next area, thus keeping paint edges wet at all times.

TOOLS: 50–60mm (2–2½ in) paintbrush, fitch, corner roller, small paint pad,

MATERIALS: Paint, clean cloth, white spirit, masking tape

CORNERS

1 When cutting in up to an already painted surface, it will be necessary to bead the paint up to the corner very precisely, in order to produce the required finish. A 50–60mm (2–2½in) brush is an ideal size for this job. Load the brush and apply a 50cm (20in) strip of paint, slightly away from the corner.

2 With the brush (now unloaded) spread the paint up to the corner junction, using the splayed edge of the bristles. Bead the paint right into the corner creating a neat, straight line. For extra precision, you may need to repeat this process two or three times to move the paint exactly into the junction.

3 In the corner of the room, or a tight angle near built-in furniture, etc, it is sometimes easiest to use a small, flat, angle-headed fitch rather than an ordinary paintbrush, however small. The finer angled bristles make it easier to get right into the corner and give a finish that is totally neat and squared.

FITTINGS

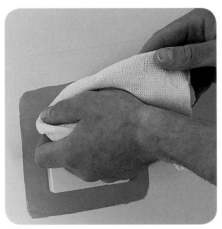

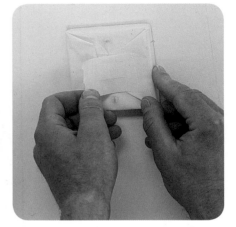

1 When cutting in around small obstacles such as electrical sockets and light switches, a fitch is often more precise and therefore easier to use than a larger brush.

2 Take care to remove any paint marks on the socket while they are still wet. Use a cloth slightly dampened with either water or white spirit, depending on the type of paint.

3 Although more time consuming, masking tape can also be used to cover fittings. If the fitting is intricate or difficult to clean, this option should be considered seriously.

4 Along an edge where both painted surfaces will be the same colour, a corner roller may be used as an alternative to cutting in with a brush. Take care not to overload the roller with paint as this will almost certainly leave unsightly roller trails and give varying thicknesses of paint that will detract from the finish.

5 Small paint pads give an excellent straight edge when cutting in to a surface of a different colour. Line up the pad's top edge against the ceiling and draw it across the wall. However, pads are not suitable if the surface is uneven or undulating: they are not very flexible and cannot bead exactly into the corner.

OVERLAPPING EDGES

Notice how, in this example, the ceiling paint was overlapped on to the wall. This is standard procedure as it is pointless to cut in precisely into a corner with both paint colours. The second colour will always cover up such overlaps, therefore saving time.

Internal doors

Doors get more wear and tear than any other painted area in the home. Solvent-based paints are most often used to cope with the needs of frequently used surfaces, because they are particularly hard-wearing. The basic rule for painting doors is to stick to a logical sequence.

Remove all door furniture before starting as this avoids having to cut in around it. This is also an ideal opportunity to either paint or clean decorative door furniture.

TOOLS: 25, 50 and 75mm (1, 2 and 3in) paintbrushes, paint kettle

MATERIALS: Paint

FLUSH DOOR

1 Mentally divide the door into eight sections, and starting in the top left-hand corner, work from left to right and downwards. Use a 50–75mm (2–3in) brush for quick coverage and therefore to avoid the danger of tide marks. Take care not to overload the wet edges of each section as this can easily lead to runs and paint sagging.

2 As each section of the door is covered, make a series of light upward strokes with the brush to lay off the paint. Once it is all complete, use a smaller brush to paint the edges of the door, plus the door frame and the architrave, using the diagram on page 79 as a guideline for exactly which areas to paint.

Colour divisions on a door and doorway

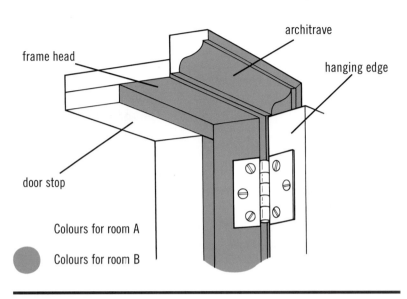

frame head

architrave

hanging edge

door stop

Colours for room A

Colours for room B

Parts of a panel door

stiles

members

panels

PANEL DOOR

1 Using a 50mm (2in) brush, begin with the top panels, doing the mouldings first. Work down, completing all the panels in sequence. Paint runs often occur at the panel corners, so it may be necessary to brush them out, returning to them several times.

2 Again starting from the top of the door, paint the central vertical stiles. Take care not to brush too far on to the horizontal members (the areas between the panels) as the vertical brush marks may show through on the final coat.

3 When the central vertical stiles are completed, paint the three horizontal members, always remembering to lay off the paint in the natural direction of the grain of the wood.

4 Paint the outer vertical stiles. Then, using a smaller brush, paint the door edges. Try to avoid getting paint on the hinges. Last, paint the door frame and architrave. Remember to wedge the door open while it dries.

Casement windows

Windows can be fiddly to paint, but by working in an organised way you can keep frustration to a minimum, and achieve a good result. Doing a thorough job on windows is particularly important: of all areas in the home, they are most affected by exterior climatic changes. Direct sunlight and condensation, as well as minor expansion and contraction of joints all take their toll.

Paint windows early in the day so they do not have to stay open all night to dry.

TOOLS: Screwdrivers, 35mm (1½in) paintbrush, paint kettle, small angle-headed brush

MATERIALS: Paint, clean cloth, masking tape

Parts of a casement window

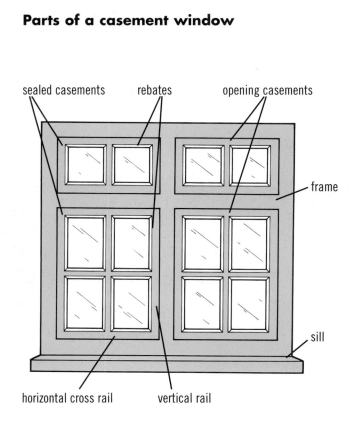

sealed casements   rebates   opening casements

frame

sill

horizontal cross rail   vertical rail

1 Remove all window furniture before painting as cutting in around it is both difficult and time consuming. On a windy day, wedge a small piece of card under the bottom of window sections that open, to stop them blowing out.

4 Having finished all sections of the window that open, paint all the non-opening parts around the panes of glass. This completes all fiddly, small sections.

METAL WINDOWS

Metal windows that are normally painted are prepared and repainted in exactly the same way as their wooden counterparts. However, if there are any patches of rust, they should be cleaned back thoroughly to the sound, bare metal and initially treated with metal primer.
  Aluminium and PVC windows are specifically designed to require very little maintenance. They should not be painted. To keep them clean and bright, wash them down during decoration with warm soapy water. Never use abrasive cleaners on either aluminium or PVC as they may scratch and disfigure the surface.

MASKING WINDOW PANES

Although time consuming, masking up individual panes is one way to keep paint off the glass surface. This is a particularly good option for the beginner, and can be discarded when your beading/cutting-in technique has been mastered. If you do mask the panes, remember to remove the tape when the top coat is still tacky, otherwise you may tear the painted surface.

2 Mentally divide the window into smaller sections, and begin by painting all the parts that open. As usual, start right at the top of the window. This example shows the small opener being painted first.

3 Paint the lower opening sections of the window. With each separate section, paint the window rebates first and work out to the cross rails and vertical rails.

5 Finish off by painting the larger parts: the outer window frame and the sill. Keep returning to the window to check for paint runs, which are especially common at the rebate–rail junctions.

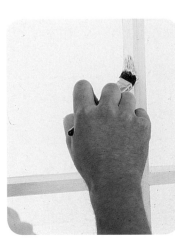

6 Painting window rebates needs a technique similar to cutting in (see page 76). Again it is necessary to bead the paint right up to the wood–glass junction. This can be made easier by using a small angle-headed brush.

Sash windows

Due to their design, sash windows appear to be difficult to paint, but if the correct sequence of painting is followed, they are as straightforward as any other painting job.

If the runners are in sound, painted condition they are best left alone, as too many coats of paint will make the window jam. It is also important to keep paint away from the sash cords, so they can run freely.

TOOLS: Fitch, 50mm (2in) paintbrush, paint kettle, window guard, window scraper

MATERIALS: Paint, masking tape

Parts of a sash window

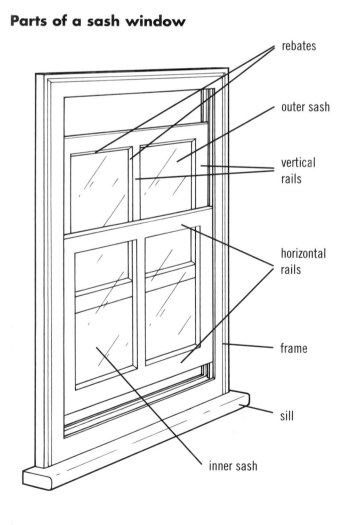

rebates

outer sash

vertical rails

horizontal rails

frame

sill

inner sash

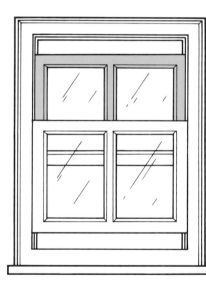

1 Open the window slightly at both top and bottom, and start by painting the top half of the outer sash rebates. Move on to the horizontal and vertical rails.

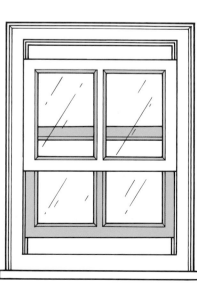

2 Raise the inner sash until it is nearly at the top of the frame and pull down the outer sash. Finish off painting the rebates, horizontal and vertical rails on the outer sash. Then paint the inner sash rebates.

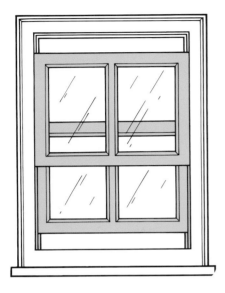

3 Leave the sashes in the same position as step 2, and finish painting the inner sash. Then paint the exposed lower runners, taking care not to touch or smudge the wet paint just applied to either of the sashes.

4 Return the window to its original position (step 1) and paint the upper runners. The top and bottom edges of the inner sash can now be painted. Finally, paint the surrounding frame and sill.

Parts of a sash window – mechanism

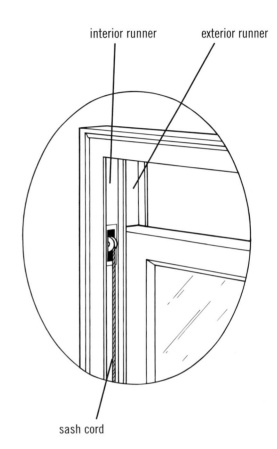

interior runner   exterior runner

sash cord

IDEAL TOOLS

Window guards
Saves time by keeping paint off the glass. Hold the guard tight up against the glass and the rebate, paint around the pane and move the guard along to the next area. Window guards are less effective on older widows, as undulating rebates and small joint variations allow paint to squeeze out under the guard's edges. Wipe it clean frequently to avoid paint build-up and smudging.

Window scraper
Handy for removing paint overspill or spray from the glass of the window once the paint has dried.

Fitch
Useful for painting the runners as it is important to keep paint clear of the sash cord, otherwise the sliding mechanism will be hampered.

Metal

Household fixtures and fittings are made from a variety of metals. For example, central-heating radiators are commonly made from ferrous metals whereas copper pipes and aluminium are non-ferrous and do not corrode as much. Window and door furniture may be made from either of these types.

Remove as much metalwork as possible from doors and windows. This will make painting both the main object and the metal fitting much easier.

TOOLS: Fitch, 37 and 50mm (1½ and 2in) paintbrushes, paint kettle, wire brush, scraper, screwdriver

MATERIALS: Heat-resistant, solvent-based and aerosol paints, wire wool, clean cloth, wooden battens

HEATED METAL SURFACES

1 Always prepare and paint an object that gets hot, when it is cold. Otherwise the paint will dry too quickly, producing an uneven, blotchy finish. On cast iron, such as a wood-burning stove or a fire surround, use a wire brush to remove any loose material, then dust off. Wipe down using a cloth dampened with white spirit to remove any remaining particles.

2 Because a cast-iron stove or fireplace may reach a very high temperature when it is being used, apply a paint specifically manufactured for heated cast-iron surfaces. Paints that are not heat resistant would burn and bubble off. A primer is not usually necessary with such specialist paints and two full-strength coats, painted or sprayed on, should be sufficient.

3 For pipes and radiators, solvent-based paints are best as most water-based paints will discolour with the heat.

DOOR AND WINDOW FITTINGS

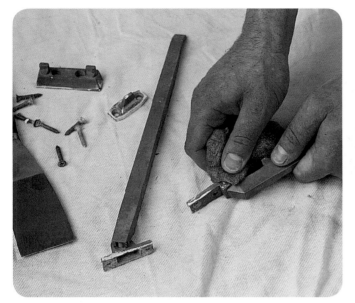

1 Tarnish and spots of paint can be cleaned off most window furniture with fine-grade wire wool. However, this method may scratch or abrade some surfaces, so try a small test area first. Alternatively, use the edge of a scraper to remove old paint.

2 Some window furniture can be rejuvenated or blended into your chosen colour scheme by being sprayed with aerosol paint. Check that the paint is suitable for the type of metal, and raise the items up on a couple of wooden battens to give access to all sides when spraying.

3 Alternatively, paint such objects using a small fitch. Placing them on a clean board will prevent them sticking to dust sheets while drying.

4 Do not paint the screws before reattaching the fitting as a screwdriver will damage the paint. Simply 'touch in' the screw heads once replaced.

CHAPTER 2

WALLPAPERING

Using wallpaper to decorate a room can be one of the most dramatic and instant ways of transforming it. Modern papers offer an almost unlimited variety of patterns and textures, allowing you to create any style, be it classical elegance, a pretty country-look or a striking, modern interior.

The essence of good wallpapering, like all decorating, lies in thorough planning and preparation. It is important to read the sections in Chapter 1, Painting Interiors that explain how to strip paper, fill ceilings and walls, clean and seal surfaces and hang lining paper before beginning to hang the wallpaper itself.

Some people find the thought of hanging wallpaper daunting, yet if you know how to go about it, you can achieve results as good as those of a professional decorator. This chapter guides you through the principal techniques, explaining how to start, how to match patterns and paper awkward joins, and helps you solve any problems that you may encounter.

Colour schemes and designs

The predominant colour of wallpaper obviously affects the atmosphere of a room. Warm colours, such as oranges or yellows, 'advance' to create a welcoming atmosphere, while cooler colours, such as greens or blues, create an impression of space and a fresh, soothing mood. Many wallpaper designs contain a number of different colours and it can be difficult to decide which is the dominant colour. In such cases, the bolder, darker colours tend to be the decisive influence.

Pattern size needs equal consideration. Large patterns tend to be the most dramatic, whereas 'busy' patterns are excellent for disguising imperfections and are generally easier for the beginner to hang, as small mistakes in paper-hanging technique are lost in the energetic design. Symmetrical papers, such as stripes, must be applied very precisely, as they tend to accentuate any faults.

◀ Large floral designs are classic decorative wallpaper patterns. Always take into account room size when using them as they can be overpowering in a small area. In rooms that are predominantly used for relaxing, large floral patterns will always give a feeling of luxury and elegance.

◄ Smaller, repetitive designs create a more active impression within a room. They help to hide imperfections, both in the wall and in paper-hanging skills, and provide excellent backdrops for paintings, ornaments and general architectural features.

► Wallpaper should always be complemented by the other colours in the room. Choose the colours of paint for woodwork carefully and always try out test patches of the paint and wallpaper before purchasing large quantities and going ahead with the decoration. Once the basic colour scheme has been selected, consider amalgamating suitable wallpaper with decorative paint effects, such as the marbled wood panels shown here.

Wallpaper finishes

Wall coverings can have various types of finish to suit different purposes and when selecting wallpaper, it is important to bear in mind the practicality of the paper for the room it is decorating. Some are more hard wearing than others, whereas some make decorative effects their main priority.

The most common categories of wallpaper are illustrated below, but there are various proprietary papers available that have slightly different characteristics. Always be sure to check the manufacturer's guidelines before hanging such papers, in order to determine their suitability.

LINING

Flat undecorated paper hung on bare wall surfaces prior to hanging decorative wallpaper.

STANDARD PATTERN

Flat wallpaper that has had a coloured design machine printed on to its surface.

WOODCHIP

Consists of two layers of paper bonded together with small chips of wood sealed between them. It provides a textured finish that is excellent for disguising rough wall surfaces. It should be painted after application, when thoroughly dried out.

BORDERS

Decorative bands of wallpaper are available in various finishes. They are generally applied horizontally at ceiling or dado level, but other uses are possible.

WALLPAPER SYMBOLS

When choosing paper, check the label symbols for factors such as washability, hanging method and pattern match.

VINYL

Popular, mass-produced vinyl papers come in a huge variety of patterns. Consist of a clear vinyl layer bonded on top of a printed pattern. Easy to keep clean and ideal in areas that need frequent cleaning. Heavy-duty vinyls are ideal for kitchens and bathrooms.

HEAVY-DUTY VINYL

A thick and very hard-wearing vinyl paper, particularly useful for areas such as kitchens and bathrooms that get damp and need constant cleaning. As it is so heavy, a strong adhesive is required or it is likely to peel off the wall.

BLOWN VINYL

Similar to ordinary vinyl except a relief pattern is mounted on the flat backing paper, producing a textured finish. The relief pattern tends to be solid or compressible and is therefore more hard-wearing than that on embossed papers (see below).

HAND-PRINTED

There are two main categories: screen printed or block printed. Both are printed one roll at a time. Pattern matching is often difficult and edges may need trimming before hanging. Usually expensive but the overall effect can be stunning.

EMBOSSED

A relief pattern is imprinted in the paper during manufacture, producing a raised decorative surface. Some are white and are usually painted once hung, while others are already decorated. Take care not to flatten the relief during application.

FLOCK

Decorated with a pattern that has been cut into fibres built into the surface. Originally these were made from silk or wool, but today synthetic equivalents are more common and easier to hang. The pattern is mounted on flat backing paper.

Materials and measuring

Wallpaper is the most expensive item on your shopping list, so you must take care when calculating the number of rolls needed. However it is not just wallpaper that is needed to complete the job, so the check-list below may help when working out your requirements, depending on the particular wall covering you have chosen.

As with tools, remember that inferior materials may not be user-friendly. Buying good-quality products may cost extra, but will be money well spent.

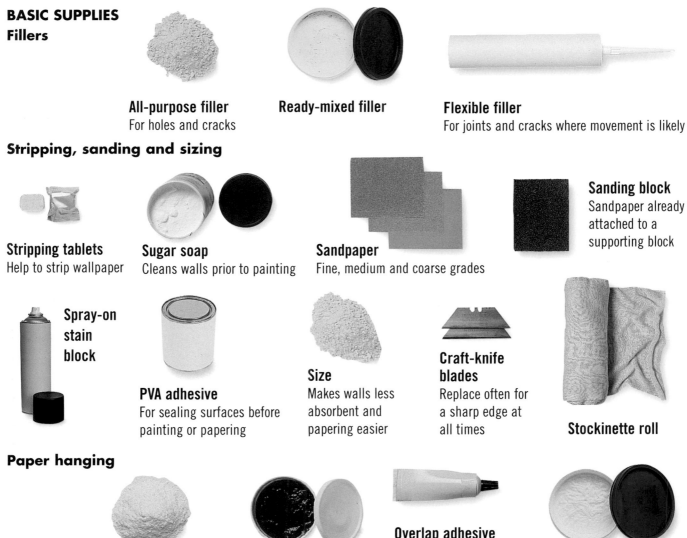

BASIC SUPPLIES

Fillers

All-purpose filler
For holes and cracks

Ready-mixed filler

Flexible filler
For joints and cracks where movement is likely

Stripping, sanding and sizing

Stripping tablets
Help to strip wallpaper

Sugar soap
Cleans walls prior to painting

Sandpaper
Fine, medium and coarse grades

Sanding block
Sandpaper already attached to a supporting block

Spray-on stain block

PVA adhesive
For sealing surfaces before painting or papering

Size
Makes walls less absorbent and papering easier

Craft-knife blades
Replace often for a sharp edge at all times

Stockinette roll

Paper hanging

Wallpaper paste

Ready-mixed paste

Overlap adhesive
Stronger than ordinary paste

Border adhesive

PAPERS

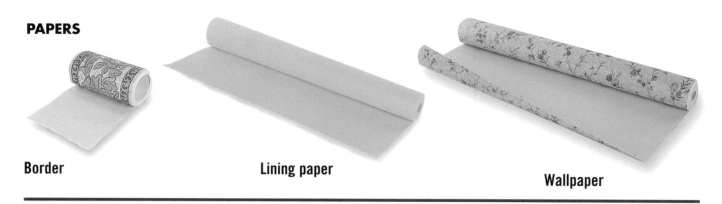

Border   **Lining paper**

Wallpaper

MEASURING UP

First, you must think about pattern repeats (see page 98). Papers with a large repeat pattern tend to produce more waste than papers with a small repeat pattern.

To find out how many rolls of wallpaper are needed, calculate the total area to be papered: see the diagram to the right, which illustrates the easiest method.

1 Measure these two lengths and multiply together to calculate the area of the ceiling.

2 Measure these two lengths and multiply them together to calculate the area of the wall to the right of the chimney breast. Use the same technique to work out the area of all other walls. Do not deduct anything for obstacles such as doors and windows, as you will need to compensate for wastage when trimming during application of the paper.

3 For wallpapering with patterned paper, add on the size of the repeat pattern to the height of the room when calculating surface area. This will allow for unavoidable wastage when applying the paper.

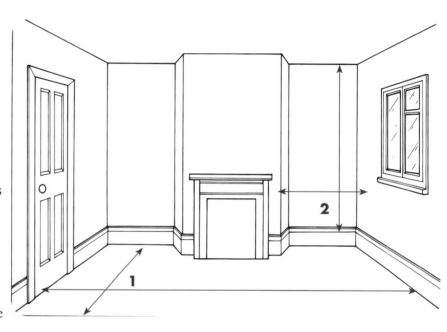

ROLLS OF WALLPAPER NEEDED

Total surface area to paper		No of rolls	For every additional 5sq m (6sq yd), add one roll of lining paper or wallpaper.
sq m	sq yd		
5	6	1	
10	12	2	
15	18	3	

Standard rolls of wallpaper are approximately 52cm x 10m = 5.2sq m (20½in x 11yd = 6¼sq yd). The excess of 0.2sq m (¼sq yd) per roll allows for both trimming and wastage.

If you are not using standard rolls, simply work out the surface area of the rolls you are using and create your own table by the same method as above.

Paper-hanging

Once a surface has been correctly prepared (see Chapter 1, Painting Interiors), the task of hanging the wallpaper itself can begin. Although there is a huge variety of papers, the vast majority are hung in the same way. This section explains the whole process, from measuring, cutting and pasting up to pattern matching and papering around difficult obstacles.

Before beginning, always read the wallpaper manufacturer's guidelines to check whether there are any specific requirements or instructions for your paper. For paste-the-paper varieties, there may be precise paste recommendations and specific instructions about the type of paste to use. These should be followed, as the chemical make-up of some pastes may be suitable only for some papers. For ready-pasted papers, there will be instructions on how long to soak the paper in order to reactivate the dry paste on its reverse side.

Also check for advice on how long the pasted paper should be left to soak. Soaking allows the paper to expand and become more pliable, making it easier to work with and less likely to bubble as it dries.

Some wallpapers may stain if the paste is allowed to dry on the patterned side, so use a clean, damp sponge to remove any excess immediately.

Where to start

Once the surface has been prepared (see Chapter 1, Painting Interiors), wallpapering can begin. Deciding where to start depends on the shape of the room and on the wallpaper design. Look at whether there is a focal point, such as a chimney breast. If so, and if you are using a large pattern, the pattern should be centralised. With smaller or free-match patterns this is not an issue, so it is best to start near a corner.

TOOLS: Step-ladder, tape measure, pencil, spirit level, hammer, nail, plumb line

MATERIALS: Wallpaper

CHECKING THE PAPER

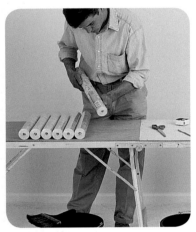

Make sure that the batch number on each roll is the same as all the others. Unwrap one of the rolls and check for any pattern imperfections or shading differences in the paper. If you do find any problems they are likely to be present in the rest of the batch. Manufacturers will generally not accept liability if more than one roll is opened, so this initial check is vital.

CENTRALISATION

Correct centralisation of wallpaper creates a well-balanced effect. The way to achieve this requires some thought, as some papers have the central pattern joining on a seam, whereas on others the central pattern will be in the middle of the length or even slightly offset.

The best method to get the pattern centred is to hold a 'dry' cut length in what will be its approximate central position above the mantlepiece, to make a pencil mark at its side and to draw a vertical guideline with the spirit level. When you come to apply this first length, use the guideline to position the paper. Then use a tape measure and spirit level to make any final adjustments to make sure the main pattern is right in the middle of the chimney breast.

Having positioned the first length, the rest of the chimney breast should be completed before the rest of the room.

▲ Poor centralisation can lead to a totally unbalanced effect.

▲ The balanced effect of good centralisation.

WHERE TO START

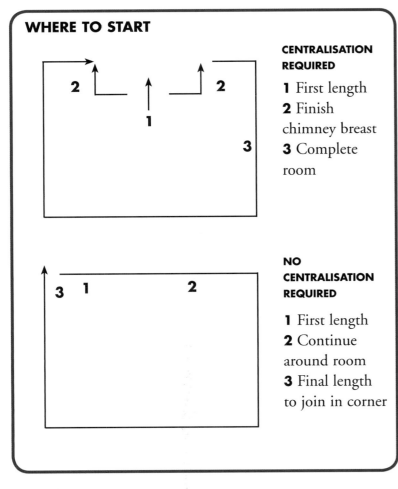

CENTRALISATION REQUIRED

1 First length
2 Finish chimney breast
3 Complete room

NO CENTRALISATION REQUIRED

1 First length
2 Continue around room
3 Final length to join in corner

USING A PLUMB LINE

A plumb line can give a reliable vertical guideline. Hammer a small nail into the wall close to the ceiling, and hang the plumb line. Make a series of pencil marks along the length of the string, and join them up with a steel rule.

NO CENTRALISATION REQUIRED

1 If pattern centralising is not required, start near an internal corner. Measure 2cm (1in) less than your wallpaper's width away from the corner, and make a mark with a pencil.

2 Place a long spirit level vertically against this mark and draw a pencil line down its complete length. This acts as a guide for your first length which should be hung on the opposite side of the line to the corner – not going into the corner itself. To the other side of the line, an overlap has been allowed for (ie, the 2cm (1in)). This will be used when you have papered all the way around the room and need to make a join in the corner (see diagram above).

Measuring and cutting

Careful and precise measuring avoids expensive mistakes (if the paper is cut too short) and unnecessary wastage (if it is cut too long). The task is made easier if you are using a free-match paper, such as vertical stripes, as no pattern matching is necessary. However, much more care is needed when dealing with patterned wallpapers, especially those with a large repeat.

TOOLS: Pasting table, tape measure, pencil, steel rule, scissors

MATERIALS: Wallpaper

MEASURING SMALL REPEATS

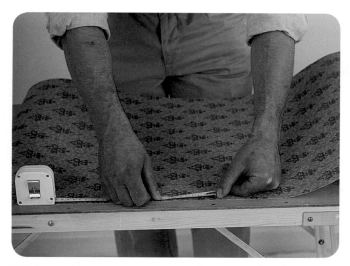

With small repeat patterns – for example of 5–10cm (2–4in) – it is best to add on to the wall height 10cm (4in) (that is, two times 5cm or 2in). This extra allows enough for trimming at each end, plus the length of the repeat. By working in this way you can cut a number of standard lengths at the start of the job, saving time by reducing the stop–start process of measuring, cutting and pasting for every length.

If you do cut a number of lengths at the beginning of the job, be sure to check first that the ceiling height is reasonably consistent all the way around the room.

MEASURING LARGE REPEATS

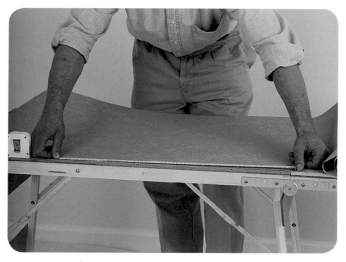

An option for larger patterns is to match the next length 'dry' to the previous length, and cut the right size, leaving enough excess just for trimming. This may be more laborious but will lead to less wastage, especially for offset patterns. Always use this technique for cutting lengths for small areas.

MEASURING PATTERN REPEAT
Most manufacturers state the size of the pattern repeat on the roll label. Whether this is the case or not, it is always best to check the size for yourself and take a precise measurement.

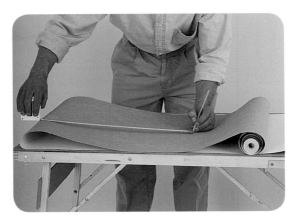

2 Unroll the paper along the pasting table. It is usually necessary to fold the paper back on itself for measuring, as most lengths will be longer than the table. Make a small mark with a pencil at the required length.

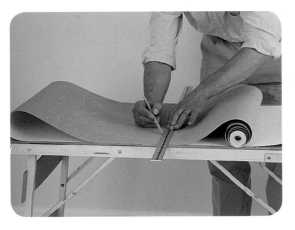

3 Always make an effort to keep the edge of the paper flush with the long edge of the table to ensure a square cut. Place a straight edge against the pencil mark and draw a line along its length, across the paper.

1 Measure the exact height of the wall from the ceiling to the top of the skirting board.

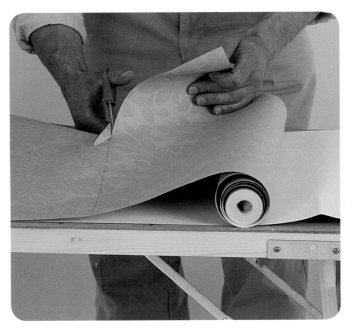

4 Use scissors to make a neat straight cut along the pencil line. It needn't be exactly even as the end of the paper will be trimmed eventually.

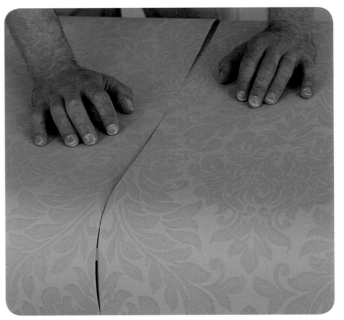

5 Prior to hanging the first length, it is worth having a 'dry run' to match the pattern as some are more subtle and less defined than others.

Pasting up

Traditional wallpapers use special wallpaper paste that is brushed on to the paper before hanging. The pasting itself is simple, but it is important to keep the length organised and tidy to avoid damaging it.

With ready-pasted papers, the dry paste on the paper is reactivated when the paper is soaked in water. When working with ready-pasted papers it is advisable to have a small amount of wallpaper paste handy as the edges may dry out.

TOOLS: Pasting table, 2 buckets, stirring stick, sponge, measuring jug, pasting brush, paper-hanging brush, scissors, wallpaper trough

MATERIALS: Wallpaper, paste, water

APPLYING WALLPAPER PASTE

1 Check the manufacturer's paste recommendations, then mix the paste (see page 48). Unroll the measured length of paper and weigh it down at one end with a paper-hanging brush. Line up the edge of the paper with the table edge; this helps prevent paste getting on the patterned side of the paper. Apply the paste evenly, brushing from the centre outwards, covering the paper with a thin film of paste.

2 Most lengths will tend to be longer than the table. Once the area of paper covering the table has been pasted, gently fold the pasted end over on itself, starting a concertina. Move the concertina of folded, pasted paper back along the table so that it rests squarely right at one end. Again, use a weight to hold down the unpasted end of the paper. Continue to paste the remainder of the length.

3 Once the entire length is pasted, continue to fold it into the concertina. Support the paper as it is folded and take care that it does not crease, as creases will be visible once it is hung. Put the completed concertina to one side for the required soaking time, marking on it the time the paper will be ready to be applied to the wall. In between pasting each length, wipe the pasting table down with a damp sponge.

READY-PASTED PAPER

 in

1 Measure and cut the paper in the usual way (see pages 98–99). On the pasting table, loosely roll up the cut length, against its natural curl from the roll, so that the reverse, pre-pasted side is outermost.

2 Fill the trough two-thirds full with cold water and position it at one end of the pasting table. Fully immerse the roll of paper in the trough and hold it under the water for the manufacturer's recommended soaking time. Agitate the roll slightly during soaking to expel any air bubbles, and to ensure all the paper comes into contact with the water.

3 Some manufacturers suggest that the paper can be drawn directly from the trough and applied to the wall, but this can be problematic. For the best results, draw the length on to a pasting table, patterned side down, allowing excess water to drain off. If further soaking is needed, carry out steps 4 and 5. If not, fold pasted sides of the length together before carrying to the wall.

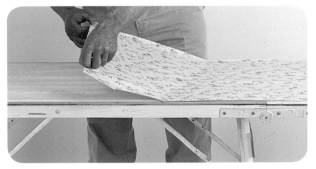

4 If extra soaking time is required, fold the top half of the paper back on itself as far as the central point of the length, pasted sides together, keeping the paper edges flush.

5 Fold the bottom half to the centre. This ensures even paste coverage and keeps the paper moist until it is ready to hang. Use a damp sponge to clean down the table between soaking the lengths.

PASTE-THE-WALL PAPERS

Some papers are designed to be hung by adding paste to the wall rather than to the paper. For the most successful results with such 'paste-the-wall' papers, coat an area of the wall slightly wider than the paper with an appropriate paste, then hang the paper directly from the roll or alternatively cut it to length first.

Hanging the first length

Before hanging the first length of paper check which way it should be hung. With some patterns the direction may at first appear not to matter; however when on the wall the direction of some patterns can be critical. Manufacturers of free-match patterns often recommend that alternate lengths should be reversed to even out any minor differences in shading, so always read the label on the paper.

It is essential to take time when hanging the first length, not only to ensure it is level but also to make certain the balance of pattern is correct, especially with large designs (see pages 96–97).

TOOLS: Pasting table, 2 buckets, sponge, pasting brush, paper-hanging brush, wallpaper trough (if needed), step-ladder, scissors

MATERIALS: Wallpaper, paste, water

1 Place the first length on the wall, next to your pencil guideline (see pages 96–97). The top of the length should be at the wall–ceiling junction with a 5cm (2in) overlap on the ceiling, for trimming. Take care, especially when unfolding concertinas, that the paper does not tear.

2 Now that the top section of the length of wallpaper is loosely attached to the wall at the correct height, slide the vertical edge of the paper into its final position next to the vertical pencil guideline.

3 Using the paper-hanging brush, firmly push the top edge of the paper into the wall–ceiling junction. Make sure the length of paper does not move from its correct vertical alignment in the process.

4 Move down the length of paper, brushing out any air bubbles or creases, working from the centre of the length outwards. Keep checking to make sure that the vertical edge of the paper is still aligned with the guideline.

5 With the top half of the paper hung securely in its final position, leave the bottom section untouched for the moment and return your attention to the wall–ceiling junction.

6 Run the blunt edge of the scissors along the paper crease in the wall–ceiling junction to give a guideline for trimming. Alternatively, a pencil may be used to make the crease.

7 Pull the paper away from the wall and trim with scissors along the creased guideline. If the ceiling is slightly uneven it is often best to trim just above the line as this gives a better finish.

8 With the paper-hanging brush, push the trimmed edge firmly back into position at the wall–ceiling junction. Add a little extra paste if the edge has dried out during trimming.

Finishing the first length

With the top half of the first length of wallpaper in position and trimmed at the top (see pages 102–103), attention can now be given to the bottom section of the wallpaper that has not been attached to the wall.

At the bottom of a wall, uneven wall–skirting-board junctions can often be a problem. To deal with them use a similar technique to that for trimming at uneven ceilings: trim slightly below the creased guideline to compensate for the undulations in the wall, and thereby produce a neater trimmed edge.

TOOLS: Pasting table, 2 buckets, sponge, pasting brush, paper-hanging brush, wallpaper trough (if needed), scissors, step-ladder, craft knife, rotary trimmer

MATERIALS: Wallpaper, paste, water

1 Once the top half of the paper is securely in place and the top edge trimmed to fit, ease the bottom half of the paper away from the wall, releasing folds if necessary.

2 Using the paper-hanging brush, continue to work downwards, again expelling air bubbles and smoothing out the paper. Firmly push the paper into the wall–skirting junction.

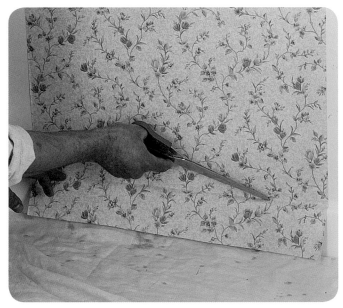

3 As with the top edge, use the scissors or a pencil to crease an exact trimming line along the junction between the wall and the skirting board. (See step 6, page 103.)

4 Pull the paper back and trim along the creased guideline. Once it is trimmed, push the edge back into the wall–skirting junction using the paper-hanging brush.

5 Finally, use a clean, damp sponge to wipe off any excess paste from the ceiling, skirting board and wallpaper surface.

IDEAL TOOLS

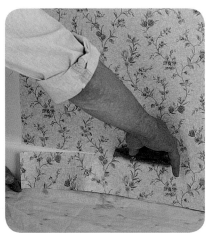

Craft knife
May be used for trimming instead of scissors. If possible, cut away from the body for obvious safety reasons. Change the blade at regular intervals to ensure a clean cut.

Rotary trimmer
Also useful for cutting paper, by running the circular blade along the guide crease. Use a dry cloth to keep the blade clean and free from paste build-up.

Pattern matching

When correctly butt-joined, most wallpaper patterns match together extremely well from one length to the next and you are rarely able to see the join.

Pattern matching can be divided broadly into three categories. Free match is where there is no specific point or design where lengths join; straight match is where there is a precise point to join lengths; and offset match is where the pattern is staggered between lengths but a precise point of join is still required. To match a precise pattern use the techniques laid out below.

TOOLS: Pasting table, 2 buckets, sponge, pasting brush, paper-hanging brush, wallpaper trough (if needed), step-ladder, scissors, craft knife, seam roller, spirit level

MATERIALS: Wallpaper, paste, water

1 Paste up the new length and place it on the wall as near to the pattern match as possible.

2 With the paper now loosely attached to the wall, slide the top half of the length flush with the edge of the previous length forming a tight butt join. At the same time, make any minor adjustments vertically to get a perfect pattern match.

3 Brush out the paper as usual, paying particular attention to the vertical edge to make sure that a neat butt join is continuing down the length of the paper and that the paper's pattern match is consistent all the way from ceiling to floor.

AVOIDING DRY EDGES

Wallpaper edges may dry out due to insufficient pasting or when tackling an awkward, time-consuming area. Keep your pasting brush handy to reapply paste where necessary.

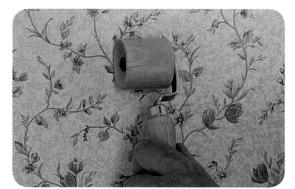

4 A seam roller may be used gently to run down the butt join to ensure good adhesion and a perfect flat finish. Do not use a seam roller with embossed papers as you may flatten the relief on the paper.

DEALING WITH PATTERN DROP

Problems with pattern-matching may occur when hanging some wallpapers, especially if hand-printed. Due to the way these papers are manufactured, some may have differences in pattern size or consistency throughout their length. By the time the paper reaches the lower part of the wall the pattern may have 'dropped'. If so, match the pattern at eye level rather than at the top, so that the area of paper that is seen most often has the best pattern match.

5 Some papers are difficult to get precisely level. On some straight-match papers the actual join may be a free match. For example, the paper may have a floral pattern in its centre, but the paper edges join on a vertical stripe design. If necessary, use a spirit level to check the horizontal line-up.

6 Free-match patterns, such as vertical stripes, are clearly the easiest to join as there is no particular match needed. However, make sure the butt join is precise, as free-match patterns will tend to show up poor joins whereas a busier floral design would disguise them.

Internal corners

All rooms have internal corners, so knowing the most successful technique to deal with them is essential. Trying to fold the wallpaper around an internal corner often causes problems with poor adhesion along the entire height of the corner crease. Furthermore, the wallpaper may be thrown off level because the corner is not totally square. Getting the paper to turn smoothly from one wall to the next is best achieved by dividing the wallpaper into two vertical strips during application.

TOOLS: Pasting table, 2 buckets, sponge, pasting brush, paper-hanging brush, wallpaper trough (if needed), step-ladder, tape measure, scissors, craft knife, spirit level, fitch

MATERIALS: Wallpaper, paste, water, overlap adhesive

1 At an internal corner, match the pattern and brush out the paper as usual, but only go as far as the corner crease. Allow the paper that has folded around the corner to loosely stick to the unpapered wall. This will make it easier to work down the length, pushing the paper into the corner junction.

2 Use the scissors to make a diagonal cut directly into the three-way junction where the wall, ceiling and corner all meet. The cut should extend as far as the actual corner itself. Make a similar cut at ground level into the junction of the skirting board and the corner.

3 With a craft knife, make a vertical cut from ceiling to floor allowing a 1–2cm (¼–½in) overlap of paper on to the unpapered wall. You may find it easier to begin and end this vertical cut using scissors.

4 Remove the offcut and place it temporarily on the unpapered wall. Return to the other part, to trim the top and bottom, and to make sure that the paper is firmly stuck down in the corner junction.

5 Move the strip of offcut paper to overlap the hung section along the length of the corner. Try to match the pattern as closely as possible. With vinyl coverings especially you may have to use a stronger adhesive to make sure that the corner overlap is stuck down properly. In such cases, pull back the paper edge along the vertical corner and apply some overlap adhesive, either straight from the tube or using a fitch. Then firmly push the paper back into its proper position.

6 To hang the second strip it is essential to use a spirit level in order to make sure you are starting the next wall with a completely vertical edge. When the position is correct, trim the top and bottom as usual. Finally, sponge down thoroughly as any overlap will always leave paste on the surface.

CHECKING THE HORIZONTAL

With some straight-match papers it may also be necessary to use a spirit level across the corner to check the horizontal line.

External corners

It is rare to find a completely square edge on an external corner. Therefore, when papering around them, it is often necessary to realign the paper to the vertical. This may be done by simply overlapping the new length on to the previous one. However, this often produces an untidy finish.

Manufacturing a butt join is the most appropriate technique to use (see pages 58–59). Having a pattern to match makes the process a little more complicated than with lining paper, but by using the following steps a professional result can be achieved.

TOOLS: Pasting table, 2 buckets, sponge, pasting brush, paper-hanging brush, wallpaper trough (if needed), step-ladder, tape measure, scissors, craft knife, steel rule, seam roller, spirit level

MATERIALS: Wallpaper, paste, water

1 When approaching an external corner, hang the paper as usual and bend the excess around the corner using the paper-hanging brush to expel bubbles and ensure good adhesion along the corner edge. Allow the section of paper which has gone around the corner to loosely attach itself in the central area of the wall. Do not apply too much pressure to the paper above or below this point as you risk tearing the paper at ceiling or ground level.

2 With a pair of scissors, make a diagonal cut precisely into the skirting–corner junction and then at the ceiling–corner junction. It will now be easier to smooth out both sections of the length on either side of the corner.

3 Trim the top and bottom and check there are no bubbles along the corner. If the new starting edge is completely vertical, you may continue to hang the next length. In many cases, however, the paper edge will be off the vertical and so some adjustment is needed. Therefore it is necessary to follows steps 4 to 8 (see right).

4 Use a craft knife to trim the paper back to the corner leaving a 4cm (1½in) overlap around the corner.

5 Hang a new length of wallpaper, covering the trimmed overlap with the edge of the new piece. However, this rough join will be quite obvious to the naked eye and risks spoiling the neatness of the finished result. The best way of solving this is to move the new length of wallpaper into such a position that although it overlaps the previous length of paper, you are also matching the pattern exactly. The width of the design will obviously affect the degree to which you may have to overlap the two lengths. Once positioned, make sure the new length is level, making a small compromise with the pattern match if necessary. Trim the new length top and bottom, as usual.

6 Place a steel rule vertically on the corner, 2cm (¾in) from the edge and use a craft knife to cut through the two lengths of overlapping paper. Move the straight edge and repeat the process, so continuing the cut from ceiling to skirting.

7 Carefully pull back this cut edge on the overlapping piece of wallpaper, and gently remove the two strips of excess paper that were stuck on top of each other. Take care not to damage the top edge, so that it makes a neat join when replaced.

8 Push the edge back together using a paper-hanging brush. You will have a perfect butt join with the pattern still matching. A seam roller can be useful here to make sure of a totally flat join. Finally, use a clean, damp sponge to clean off excess paste.

Doors and obstacles

Papering around any obstacle that stands out from the wall, such as a door, window or fireplace, calls for skilful trimming in order to obtain a neat finish.

Part of the technique involves knowing the directions in which to make the cuts, but for a completely successful finish, a sharp craft knife is absolutely vital. To keep the knife's edge sharp it is essential to keep the blade free from wallpaper paste and to change it at regular intervals.

TOOLS: Pasting table, 2 buckets, sponge, pasting brush, paper-hanging brush, wallpaper trough (if needed), step-ladder, scissors, craft knife

MATERIALS: Wallpaper, paste, water, clean cloth

FIREPLACE

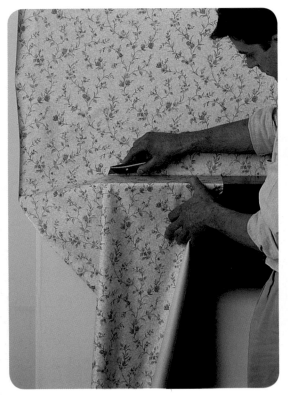

1 Allow the paper to flap over the top of the fireplace and push the paper into the wall–mantlepiece junction with the paper-hanging brush. Use a craft knife to cut from the top corner of the fireplace along the creased edge.

2 Put a finger on the corner of the cut and pick up the paper flap, gently moulding it into the angles with the paper-hanging brush. Make a series of right-angled cuts into the finely detailed areas.

3 Carefully trim each of the small flaps using a craft knife, taking care not to damage or scratch the mouldings underneath the paper.

4 Smooth the paper into its final position. Remove any excess paste from the fireplace with a damp sponge to avoid any discoloration.

DOOR

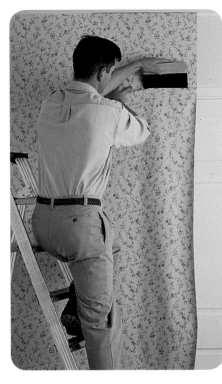

1 When the papering arrives at the door, match the pattern at a high level and then allow the remainder of the length to fall loosely over the door architrave. Using the paper-hanging brush, push the paper firmly into the top of the architrave.

2 Use your finger to mark the point where the corner of the architrave meets the wall, and using the scissors, make a diagonal cut towards this point. As you near the final point, move your finger back slightly to take the weight of the paper.

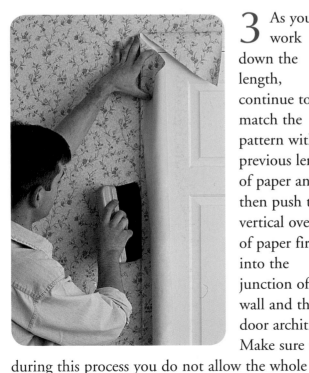

3 As you work down the length, continue to match the pattern with the previous length of paper and then push the vertical overlap of paper firmly into the junction of the wall and the door architrave. Make sure that during this process you do not allow the whole length to move, thus breaking the pattern match with the previous piece of paper.

4 Trim the two flaps with a craft knife. Use the blade at a 45-degree angle to the surface of the wall, keeping as steady a hand as possible. By making the cut slightly on to the architrave surface you will find it easier to keep a straight line as many junctions between wood and plaster are often uneven. Remember to wipe the excess paste off the woodwork immediately.

Recessed windows

Tackling a recessed window combines many of the techniques already described in this chapter. However, particular attention must be given to the order of applying the paper. It is also vital to make sure that all edges are stuck down firmly as, of all areas in the home, this is where wallpaper can be subjected to condensation problems or a wide range of temperatures.

Although a great deal of care is required to produce a neat finish around such an obstacle, beginners may take comfort in the fact that most of the joins needed will often be obscured by curtains or rails.

TOOLS: Pasting table, 2 buckets, sponge, pasting brush, paper-hanging brush, wallpaper trough (if needed), step-ladder, tape measure, scissors, craft knife, steel rule, seam roller

MATERIALS: Wallpaper, paste, water

1 When the papering arrives at the window, pattern match the length as normal and allow the paper to drop over the window recess. Make sure the area of wallpaper to the top and side of the recess is firmly stuck down in position.

2 Make two horizontal cuts back to the corners. Cut at the bottom using the window sill as a guide, then at the top, along the recess edge. Do not allow the paper to tear under its own weight. Attach the flap loosely to the wall of the recess.

3 Use the scissors to make a series of right-angled cuts into the profile of the bottom corner of the sill. This will then allow the paper to be moulded around and under the sill so that the bottom half of the length can be positioned and trimmed.

4 You may now use the same technique as described for external corners on pages 110–111 to bend the flap of paper around and into the recess. Push the paper firmly into the junction between the wall and the window frame and trim all areas as usual.

5 Cut the next length to extend from the ceiling around the top of the recess to the top of the frame. Hang it overlapping the previous length, matching the pattern. Mark the recess corner with your finger and make a diagonal cut to this point.

6 Now make a manufactured butt join. Use a steel rule and a craft knife to cut a diagonal line through the area where the two pieces overlap. Make sure the line goes through the busiest part of the pattern to disguise the join as much as possible.

7 Peel back the paper and discard the top section of the first length. Remove the bottom section of the new length, and push the pieces back together to produce a perfect butt join.

8 Bend the remaining flap around the top recess holding the paper at the recess corner to avoid tearing. Notice that in step 5 a diagonal cut was made. This is to enable you to tuck a small overlap of this section behind the flap on the side recess wall, thus producing a neat finish. Finally, trim and clean all areas with a damp sponge. Complete the rest of the window in the same way.

Stairwells

The primary concern when working in stairwells is safety. To provide a stable platform it is possible to hire scaffold towers which are designed to be erected in stairwells, but you can build your own working platform with a little ingenuity. Make sure that any planks used are rigid enough to bear your weight, and tie them to the ladders with rope.

As you are working with long lengths of paper, it is much easier to complete the job with two people.

TOOLS: Ladders, planks, rope, paper-hanging equipment, spirit level, tape measure, scissors, craft knife

MATERIALS: Wallpaper, paste, water, masking tape, stockinette roll

MAKING A PLATFORM

Secure planks to the step-ladder and ladder(s) with rope to avoid any slippage.

Make sure that the plank is sturdy; scaffolding planks are the best for this purpose. If you are bridging a gap of 1.5m (5ft) or more, tie two planks together, one on top of each other, for extra strength.

For spans that are longer than 2.4–3m (8–10ft) extra support should be used in the middle of the plank. Combination ladders, where one side can be made longer than the other, are excellent for setting up on steps.

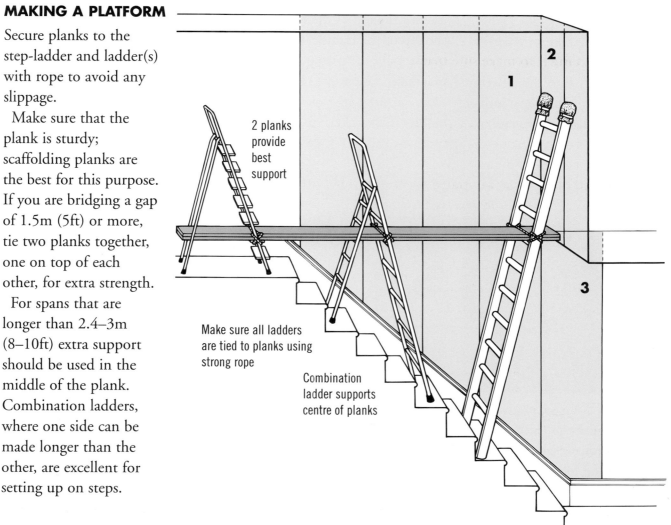

2 planks provide best support

Make sure all ladders are tied to planks using strong rope

Combination ladder supports centre of planks

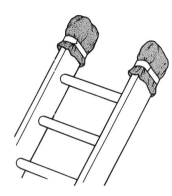

PROTECTING THE WALL

To avoid damaging new paper or a bare surface, pad the ends of the ladder. Use some stockinette roll or any soft cloth, held in place with masking tape.

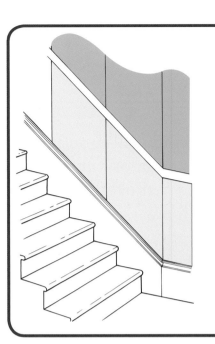

DIVIDED WALLS

The bottom levels of paper are the most likely to get dirty and receive the most physical abuse. By using two papers or even painting the lower section of wall, you can avoid having to redecorate the entire hallway and can tackle just the bottom section instead.

ORDER OF WORK

Start hanging the paper with the longest length. It is important to make sure that your first length is perfectly vertical as a minute stray from vertical at the top is hugely increased by the time you reach the bottom of the length. To find the vertical, it may help to use a plumb line.

By working up the stairs as illustrated right, measuring subsequent lengths is made much more straightforward than if you worked down the stairs.

Once you have completed all the lengths (to the left of point 1, in the diagram left), and on the opposite wall, if required, it is then possible to dismantle the platform, leaving just the long ladder in order to hang the lengths from point 2 (see left).

As illustrated above, padding on the ends of the ladder is vital to prevent damaging the wallpaper.

Finally, remove the ladder and continue from point 3 to finish the other walls downstairs. Continue papering on the upper floor, if required.

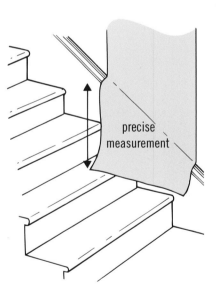

precise measurement

PAPERING UP STAIRS

The shape of walls above staircases can waste a great deal of paper. It is easy to make measuring mistakes if you work down the stairs as you can only make a rough measurement as to where the paper end will drop. To avoid expensive mistakes it is much easier to work from the longest length back up the stairs, as described and illustrated left.

PATTERN OF PAPER

Certain patterns have particular effects in stairwells. Stripes will appear to raise the height of the walls. A busy pattern, which by nature usually matches well, will reduce the risk of pattern-drop problems or unavoidable overlaps on such a wide, open area.

Wall-mounted fittings

It is difficult to paper around wall-mounted fittings such as lights and central-heating radiators, and it is usually easier to remove them. However, removing a radiator may be problematic due to old pipework and connections that have seized up.

Wall lights should be easy to take down, but if they prove difficult to move, be careful to keep paste off brass and other fittings as it will quickly tarnish them.

For guidelines on how to trim around electrical wall sockets and switches, see pages 64–65.

TOOLS: Pasting table, 2 buckets, sponge, pasting brush, paper-hanging brush, wallpaper trough (if needed), step-ladder, tape measure, craft knife, scissors, pencil, radiator roller, screwdriver

MATERIALS: Wallpaper, paste, water, electrical insulating tape

RADIATORS

1 Allow the paper to fall over the top of the radiator, making sure that the top section of the length is correctly joined with the previously hung piece. Pull the paper back slightly and using a pencil, mark the location of the supporting bracket.

2 Make a vertical cut with scissors from the bottom of the paper, just up to the pencil mark. Paste from the paper will inevitably get on the radiator, but it can be wiped off when you have finished fixing the paper to the wall behind.

3 Using a radiator roller, push the paper into position on either side of the supporting bracket. Trim the paper below the radiator, as usual, and wipe off any excess paste from all surfaces. Repeat steps 1–3 when papering around the other bracket.

LIGHT FITTINGS

1 Turn off the electricity supply at the mains or consumer unit. Unscrew the wall-mounted fitting, taking care to support its weight until it is free of the wall.

2 Using electrical insulating tape, cover the exposed wires. Replace the supporting screws in the wall. It may be helpful to draw a diagram of the wire layout to assist you when replacing the fitting.

3 Allow the paper to fall over the area. Mark the position where the wire protrudes from the wall, using a pencil. With scissors, make a small cut in the paper on this mark, then carefully thread the wire through the hole.

4 Using a paper-hanging brush, smooth out the paper, allowing the wall screws to break through the paper surface. Trim the rest of the paper as necessary. Allow the paper to dry out completely before replacing the fitting.

Ceilings

The technique used to wallpaper a ceiling is similar to that used when lining a ceiling (see pages 52–53). Pattern considerations make it essential that the paper is squared up correctly on the ceiling. Again, it is much easier to paper a ceiling with two people, but it is still perfectly possible to tackle it on your own provided you take time and care, especially when applying the first length.

When using an embossed paper on ceilings or walls, as illustrated here, take care not to apply too much pressure to the paper surface as you may flatten the relief.

TOOLS: Trestles, planks, pasting table, 2 buckets, sponge, pasting brush, paper-hanging brush, wallpaper trough (if needed), scissors, tape measure, chalk line, hammer, craft knife

MATERIALS: Wallpaper, paste, water, 2 nails, chalk

1 Decide on the direction in which to hang the lengths, and set up planks and trestles. Measure out from the side wall the exact width of the paper, minus a 2.5cm (1in) overlap on to the wall. Do this for both ends of the first length. This allows for any ceiling–wall junction unevenness and for trimming.

2 A chalk line, snapped against the ceiling, is ideal for providing a long, straight guideline for hanging the first length accurately. At each end of the measured width, hammer a small nail into the ceiling. Do not knock the nails in too far or removal will be difficult.

3 Apply some ordinary coloured chalk to a chalk line. If you do not have a proper chalk line, some household string will do as long as the chalk dust loosely bonds with the string. Attach the line to the nails. Make sure that the line is taut.

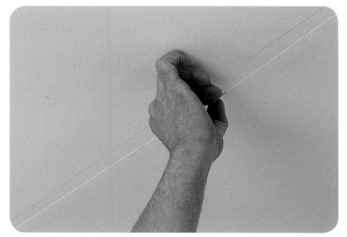

4 Go to the centre of the plank, pull the line down approximately 5–10cm (2–4in) from the ceiling and then release it. This snapping action leaves a straight chalk line on the ceiling. Remove the line and nails.

5 Now that the guideline is in place, begin papering at the junction between the wall and the ceiling using the chalk guideline to position the edge of the first length precisely. This should give the planned 2.5cm (1in) overlap on to the wall as measured in step 1.

6 Use the paper-hanging brush to brush out bubbles and push the paper into the wall–ceiling junction. For further instructions on trimming see pages 52–53. You will find that once this first length is in position, subsequent lengths are far less time consuming.

Borders

The appearance of a room can be dramatically changed by a border, whether applied over wallpaper or a painted surface. At whatever height you choose to hang the border it is important to ensure that it is level or it may give an unbalanced effect to the rest of your decoration. Border adhesive tends to dry very quickly so always tackle one wall at a time and never attempt to go around the entire room with one length.

TOOLS: Pasting table, bucket, sponge, small pasting brush, paper-hanging brush, spirit level, scissors, tape measure, pencil

MATERIALS: Border, border adhesive, water

1 Measure from the top of the skirting up to the height at which you want the top or bottom of the border to hang and make a mark with a pencil. From this mark use a spirit level to draw a guideline right around the room. However, do not press too hard with the pencil or the line may show through the border once it is hung.

2 Measure the width of the first wall, adding a 5cm (2in) overlap at each end. Cut this length and using a small brush add the border adhesive to the reverse side. Concertina the border (see page 51) and leave it to soak for the required time.

3 Starting in one corner of the first wall, apply the border to the wall. Let the 5cm (2in) overlap go around the corner and on to the adjacent wall. The border edge should follow the pencil line, but slightly overlapping it so that the pencil marks will not be visible once the border is hung.

SELF-ADHESIVE BORDERS
These are easy to use, as you simply peel away the backing paper. They obviously produce less mess but it is difficult to adjust the position of some once they are stuck down.

4 Continue along to the other corner, brushing out any air bubbles and making sure that the border is perfectly level. Again, allow the 5cm (2in) overlap to go round the corner.

5 In both corners, use scissors to trim the paper back to leave a 5mm (¼in) overlap on to the adjacent wall. Then sponge down the entire length to remove any excess adhesive.

6 Pattern match the end of the next piece of dry border to the corner you have just finished hanging. Then roll out the dry border along the length of the wall, to find out the length you need, and again add a single 5cm (2in) overlap (not 10cm (4in) as in step 2). Paste up the new length and apply to the wall as before. Take care to match the pattern in the corner by allowing the new length to overlap on top of the old length. Once positioned correctly, score down the crease of the corner using scissors, peel back the new length and cut directly along the creased line.

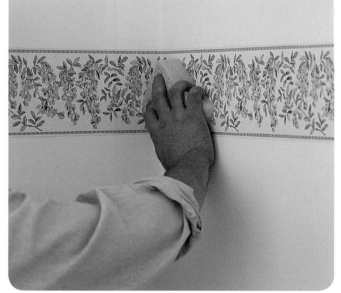

7 Push the border back into position using a sponge to remove excess adhesive. The small overlap that was left on the previous length reduces any danger of a line or gap appearing in the corner, especially if the corner junction is not square. The overlap therefore improves the finish and is practically invisible. Continue to hang the rest of the border using the same techniques.

Divides and mitring

Borders can be hung to provide a decorative divide between different wallpapers; in a rectangle to produce shapes like panelling; or to highlight the features of a room, such as framing a window. To achieve a neat finish it is necessary to join the horizontal and vertical lengths with a mitred join. Because you will not be able to pattern match the border exactly on each join, choose the border carefully; busy florals tend to hide any inconsistencies in pattern match better than symmetric designs.

TOOLS: Pasting table, bucket, sponge, small pasting brush, paper-hanging brush, step-ladder, scissors, tape measure, pencil, craft knife, steel rule, spirit level

MATERIALS: Border, border adhesive, water

BORDER DIVIDES

1 Using a border to separate two different wallpapers can be very effective. Before hanging the wallpaper make a pencil line on the wall at the height where the centre of the border is to hang. Hang the two papers at the same time with each overlapping the pencil line by 5cm (2in).

2 Using the level of the pencil line on the wall as a guide cut through the overlapping paper. Remove the excess strips, creating a manufactured butt join. (This is a similar technique to that shown on pages 110–111.)

3 Hang the border using the technique described on pages 122–123. If you are lucky the pattern of the wallpaper will give you a ready-made level guideline to follow, eliminating the need to make a pencil line.

CREATING WALL PANELS WITH A MITRED FRAME
For wall panels the first, top measurement should be exactly the length of the top side of the panel required. Then continue to make precise measurements for the other three sides. This will ensure consistency with any other panels you apply. However, when applying a single frame the top horizontal guideline is all that is needed.

MITRED FRAME

1 Use a pencil and spirit level to make a horizontal guideline above the window to the correct width of the finished border. Cut the first length of border 5cm (2in) longer than the exact length required. Paste the border as described on pages 122–123 and apply to the wall following the pencil guideline. Make sure that there is an equal overlap of border on each side of the frame.

2 Cut the first vertical length, again 5cm (2in) longer than the height required. Paste it and hang it on the wall using the spirit level to maintain an exact vertical line. The overlap that has been allowed is useful in order to try and adjust the pattern so that you will be cutting through the busiest part of the design in step 3, making the join less visible.

3 Hold a steel rule at a 45-degree angle from the external to the internal corner of the border frame. Cut through the two lengths of border using a craft knife.

4 Peel back the two long strips of border and remove the excess flaps that are stuck to the wall. Brush the paper firmly back into position to create a perfect mitred join.

5 Hang the second vertical length of border and then last, the bottom horizontal length. Be sure to keep removing excess adhesive from all surfaces with a clean, damp sponge.

CHAPTER 3

WALL TILING

There is no better testimony to the usefulness and durability of ceramic wall tiles than the fact that they have been popular for centuries. They provide a hard-wearing, waterproof surface, that is both decorative and functional, and can be applied to a variety of wall surfaces, including plaster, plasterboard, cement render, plywood, painted surfaces and even over old ceramic tiles.

Good tiling requires care and patience, as well as an understanding of what you are doing and why. This chapter explains all the necessary techniques, including the vital planning and preparation stages, in step-by-step detail, giving you all the information that you need to tile a wall successfully. If you follow the steps carefully, there is no reason why you should not achieve excellent results.

Classical influence

The use of tiles and mosaics in bathrooms dates back many, many centuries. They are the most practical means of giving the walls – and floors – an attractive, waterproof surface. Used with care, and combined with carefully chosen bathroom fittings, they can give a bathroom a timeless, classical look.

One important consideration, regardless of the style of your bathroom, is to use large tiles when tiling a large area, such as a wall or even a complete room. These produce a far less 'busy' looking surface, and in a small room actually help to make it look larger. Reserve small tiles for small areas such as splashbacks.

▶ White tiles with simple black patterns have been used to link the white and black tiled areas visually.

▼ Accents of colour in an expanse of white tiles focus the eye, preventing the area from looking cold and uninteresting.

▲ Although it is generally much better to use large tiles when tiling a large area, small mosaics can also be very effective. The reason for this is that the individual mosaic pieces are so small that the eye does not immediately recognise them individually and the wall takes on a pleasing mottled appearence.

Another advantage of small mosaics is that they are ideal for tiling a curved surface.

▲ By using a contrasting colour of tile to form a floor-to-ceiling panel behind the basin, warmth and interest have been added to this bathroom. The inset tiles below the lights on the adjacent wall provide additional visual interest and prevent this area from being dominated by the darker area.

▶ Although the strong colour of these splashback tiles contrasts effectively with the tiles used throughout the rest of the bathroom, the edge of the panel has been given further definition by adding patterned dado/border tiles.

Simple patterns

The wide variety of tiles available makes it possible to match any decor scheme imaginable: from simple rustic to high-tech futuristic. No matter what the style of the room, there will be tiles to fit right in.

Arranging the tiles in simple patterns can be a particularly effective way of giving visual interest to tiled areas. One frequently used technique is to fix the tiles diagonally, rather than horizontally or vertically. Combinations of tiling patterns also work well.

◄ Half-tiling bathroom walls can often be as effective as tiling them completely, and it reduces the overall cost of the job. Tiles should be fixed to the wall up to dado (waist) height – or at least high enough above the basin to provide an effective splashback.

Although you can leave the edges of the top tiles showing – if glazed – it is much more effective to add a proper dado of some form. You can use dado tiles or, as here, a wooden moulding.

▲ A horizontal row of alternating blue and pale green tiles at worktop level and a simple diamond motif add interest to a tiled splashback.

▲ A splashback can often accommodate a pattern or colour combination that would be too overwhelming on a larger scale. Here, two strong blues, make a striking but simple visual statement.

◄ To add visual interest to this tiled splashback, the taller area of tiles behind the hob has been given a simple diagonally tiled panel outlined by moulded dado tiles.

Tiles and materials

For the widest selection of tiles, visit a tile specialist, who will also be able to advise you on the quantities you need together with any other essential materials. An important consideration when choosing tiles is whether you want to have glazed or unglazed edges. With the latter, unless the area that you want to tile is bordered in some way on all four sides, you will need to use special border tiles, plastic tile trim or a wooden moulding to finish the edges.

The materials required for tiling will depend on the job itself. In some cases, all you will need, aside from the tiles themselves, is the appropriate adhesive, grout and tile spacers.

TILES

Standard

Ceramic wall tiles offer a wide range of colours, patterns and sizes from which to choose. Smaller tiles are best used for splashbacks rather than large ones. Some of these have been fired to higher temperatures than ordinary wall tiles and have a hard, glazed surface suitable for kitchen worktop use.

Borders and dados

Border and dado tiles come in a variety of sizes, colours, patterns and shapes. Although normally fixed in horizontal bands to break up or frame a large expanse of plain tiles, they can also be used vertically. Those with moulded relief patterns will bring an added dimension of shape to a scheme.

Inserts

An insert is designed to fit at the point where the corners of four tiles meet. They provide a simple means of breaking up a large expanse of plain tiles. Special tiles with one corner cut off accommodate the inserts.

Insets and features

Inset tiles come in standard sizes. They can be fixed at random or in a pattern among plain tiles to add visual accents. Two or more tiles sometimes fit together to make a larger picture.

Hand-painted

Hand-painted tiles offer unique motifs and make wonderful insets. No two hand-painted designs will ever be the same, which is part of their appeal.

MATERIALS

Plastic sealing strip
For finishing external corners of walls and edges of splashbacks when using tiles with unglazed edges

Quadrant tiles
Narrow tiles, with a curved profile, used to make a waterproof joint between the bath and wall.

Clean cloth   **Sponge**

Cross-shaped tile spacers
Ensures uniform joints between tiles.

Glasspaper
For sanding down filler when preparing walls

Bath trim
Makes a waterproof joint between the bath and wall, the tiles being fixed over its vertical lip.

Plastic scouring pad
Removes excess epoxy grout from worktop tiles.

Silicone carbide paper
For keying surface of old tiles for new tile adhesive.

Sanding block

ADHESIVE

Adhesive for fixing ceramic tiles to walls is available both ready-mixed, and in powder form for mixing with water. The former is more convenient to use, but the latter is less expensive and may be worth considering for a large job. Various quantities are available, and coverage is specified on the container.

There are two basic types of adhesive:

All-purpose
A water-resistant adhesive suitable for use in kitchens and bathrooms. Some all-purpose adhesives can also be employed as grout, but make sure that this is specified on the container before using it in this way.

Waterproof
Use in areas where the tiles are subjected to regular and substantial soaking in water, such as shower cubicles.

GROUT

Grout comes as a powder for mixing with water or ready-mixed. A hardener must be added to epoxy grout before it can be used. White grout is the most common, but a range of colours is also available. The container will specify the coverage you can expect. Various types are available:

Standard
Use where the tiles are unlikely to come into contact with water.

Water-resistant
For splashbacks and general kitchen and bathroom tiling.

Waterproof
Use where the tiles will be subjected to regular and substantial soaking, such as shower cubicles.

Epoxy
A very hard grout that is waterproof and will not harbour germs. Use for kitchen worktops.

Types of surface

In many cases, you may want to tile a wall that was previously painted or papered. Tiles can be applied directly over gloss and emulsion paint, provided the underlying plaster and the paint itself are sound. The minimum of preparation work will be necessary prior to tiling. However, walls that have an old-fashioned distemper finish should be stripped completely, as distemper is notoriously unstable. Wash it off with water and a little wallpaper stripper, then seal the surface with a stabilising solution.

Old wallpaper should be stripped completely. Whether you use the traditional soak-and-scrape method, as illustrated below, or a steam stripper (see pages 34–35), make sure the wall has dried completely before tiling.

TOOLS: Bucket, sponge, scraper, sanding block, 100mm (4in) paintbrush, hammer, cold chisel, small trowel, wooden batten

MATERIALS: Stripping tablets, water, sandpaper, sugar soap, stabilising solution/tile adhesive primer, ready-mixed mortar/one-coat plaster, silicone carbide paper

PREPARING THE WALL

1 If the wall was papered originally, soak the paper with a solution of wallpaper stripper, and scrape it off. Vinyl types should be peeled off and their backing paper stripped to expose the plaster. Similarly, remove any lining paper.

2 On painted surfaces, rub down any flaking paint with coarse sandpaper until you have a sound finish. To help the tiles stick to the wall, key the paint by scoring with a scraper. Wash down with a sugar-soap solution to remove dust and grease.

3 Whatever the surface, it should be sealed with a proprietary stabilising solution, such as PVA sealant or tile adhesive primer. Dilute this and apply according to the manufacturer's instructions. Allow to dry completely.

OLD CERAMIC TILES

You can retile directly on top of existing ceramic tiling, provided the tiles are firmly attached to the wall and offer a reasonably flat surface. If possible, arrange the positions of the new tiles so that they overlap the joints of the old; this will produce a stronger result.

1 If any of the original tiles are broken, loose or hollow-sounding, carefully rake out the surrounding grout using a nail and chip them out with a hammer and cold chisel. Dampen the wall behind and fill the recess with either mortar or plaster.

2 Make the mortar or plaster exactly level with the surrounding tiles by working a small wooden batten across the area with a gentle sawing action. If necessary, fill any depressions with more mortar or plaster. Check that it is level again and allow it to dry completely.

3 Although the surface of ceramic tiles should provide a sound enough base for the new tiles, you can make doubly sure by rubbing them down with silicone carbide paper. This will scratch the glaze, providing an effective key for the tile adhesive.

4 Finally, wash the tiles down thoroughly with soapy water to remove all traces of dust and grease. Make sure they are completely dry before beginning to add the new tiles.

Cracks and holes

It is essential to have a flat surface on which to apply tiles. Although tile adhesive can accommodate depressions in the wall of up to 6mm (¼in), any significant undulation will be reflected in the finished tiled surface. It is a good idea to check the flatness of the wall with a long wooden straight edge, running it up the wall and along it.

Small bumps can be hammered down and any resulting depressions filled. Low areas can also be filled; if necessary, deepen them and replaster. If the wall is very uneven, it may pay to apply a skim of fresh plaster or even to panel the wall with plasterboard.

Minor cracks in plaster can be left, but fill large ones. Any loose areas of plaster should be hacked off and the area replastered or filled.

TOOLS: Steel rule, hammer, dusting brush, filling knife, old 25mm (1in) paintbrush, small trowel, bolster chisel, steel float, short wooden batten, sanding block

MATERIALS: Filler, one-coat plaster/ready-mixed mortar, coarse sandpaper, masonry nails, stabilising solution/tile adhesive primer

1 Major cracks in plasterwork should be filled. First, work the corner of the filling knife blade along the crack to undercut the edges (so that the filler can grip well), then brush out any loose debris with a dusting brush. Use an old paintbrush to dampen the crack and press filler into it with the knife. Dampen the straight edge of the blade and use it to level the filler with the surrounding wall.

2 Filler won't dry properly if it is applied too thickly, so deep holes must be filled in two or more stages. Use a small trowel to insert an initial layer, using the point to work it down into the crevices at the bottom of the hole.

4 Do not worry about minor damage to external corners, as the tiles and/or corner trim will bridge any slight gap. However, where substantial portions of the plaster are missing, the corner should be built up with filler or one-coat plaster. Temporarily nail a batten to one edge to provide a support for the filler.

3 When the first layer of filler has dried, add another layer with a filling knife, pressing it in well and striking it off level with the surrounding plaster.

5 Check that the plaster is in contact with the wall by rapping it with your knuckles; where it has come away from the backing you will hear a hollow sound. Chop these areas away with a bolster chisel and hammer, undercutting the edges. Then fill with one-coat plaster or mortar, levelling it with the surrounding plaster using a wooden batten.

6 Allow any filled areas to dry completely, then rub them down with coarse sandpaper wrapped around a sanding block. You do not need to achieve the perfect surface that you would need for painting, but the filled area must be level with the surrounding surface. Finally, seal the wall with a stabilising solution or tile adhesive primer.

Boxing in and panelling

Wherever possible, pipes that run down or along walls should be concealed by boxing them in, and the resulting box tiled as usual. You can panel the box with plasterboard, MDF, or marine-grade plywood where damp conditions are expected. A rigid construction is essential to avoid cracking of the grout between the tiles, so use screws rather than nails to hold it together. Where the box conceals a hot water pipe, insulate the pipe to contain the heat; otherwise, it may cause the wood to shrink, again causing cracking.

All wooden surfaces should be sealed with a solvent-based primer prior to tiling.

TOOLS: Tape measure, pencil, saw, bradawl, electric drill, wood bit, masonry bit, countersink bit, screwdriver

MATERIALS: 25 x 25mm (1 x 1in) or 50 x 25mm (2 x 1in) battens, 12 or 19mm (½ or ¾in) marine-grade plywood/MDF/ plasterboard,countersunk screws, wall plugs, silicone sealant

CONCEALING PIPES

1 Where pipes run down a corner of the room, fix 25mm (1in)-square vertical battens to each wall, securing them with countersunk screws driven into wall plugs. Position the battens so that the size of the finished box will not require any cut tiles.

2 Cut two sections of 19mm (¾in)-thick marine-grade plywood or MDF to the correct size, and butt-joint them along their outer edges, using countersunk screws. Then screw the assembled panels to the battens already fixed on the wall.

BOXING PIPES

A separate framework will not be necessary if you use board butt-joined at the corner, screwed to battens.

PANELLING A BATH

1 A bath can be made to look an integral part of a bath-room if it is given a tiled surround. The procedure is essentially the same as boxing in pipes: a wooden framework is built around the bath and panelled in ready for tiling. Construct a framework around the bath, using 50 x 25mm (2 x 1in) wooden battens. Screw them to the adjacent walls and floor to provide a rigid structure. Many acrylic and fibreglass baths have wooden reinforcing around the edge, and the frame can be screwed to this as well. Alternatively, make the framework slightly lower than the bath so that you can tile under the lip.

2 Panel the framework with 12mm (½in) marine-grade plywood, attaching it with countersunk screws. Make sure the screw heads are below the surface, as otherwise they will get in the way of the tiles and make the surface uneven.

3 At the tap and waste outlet end, make up an access panel, or purchase a ready-made double-lipped access panel, securing it with magnetic catches. The panel must be large enough for you to reach all the plumbing. After tiling, disguise the edges of the panel with silicone sealant, which will still allow the panel's removal.

COVERING BARE BRICK WALLS

To tile a bare brick wall it can be plastered, but it will be quicker to panel it with plasterboard, 12mm (½in) plywood or MDF sheets.

First, fix framework to the wall, using 50 x 25mm (2 x 1in) vertical battens spaced no further apart than 30cm (12in). In addition, horizontal battens should run along the top and bottom of the wall. Frame window and door openings completely.

Screw the battens to the wall, using a long straight edge and a spirit level to ensure that they are all in line from top to bottom and perfectly vertical. If necessary, pack behind them with scraps of wood. Then fix the panels using countersunk screws.

When using plywood as a base for tiling, choose a waterproof type in case moisture should seep through any of the joints. This is essential when constructing a shower cubicle.

Planning

Once you have decided on the types of tile you want to use, you need to work out just how many you will require. The first task is to determine the area to be tiled, whether it is a simple splashback or a complete room. The easiest way of doing this is to draw up a plan, mark all the relevant dimensions on it and calculate the area from them. Tiles are sold in various quantities in packs, boxes and cartons, and your supplier will be able to advise you on the quantity needed.

Remember to allow extra for cutting in at the edges and for breakages. For an area of 5sq m (5sq yd), buy ten per cent more than you need; for a larger area, add an extra five per cent. Work out the tiling pattern: where you will place inset tiles or feature panels, and whether you will want a dado or border tiles. With the latter, you need to know the total length required, rather than the area.

DRAWING A PAPER PLAN

Draw a plan of the wall, or portion of wall, to be tiled. If you are tiling a whole room, draw each wall separately. There is no need to make the drawings accurate in terms of scale, simply use them as a visual guide to the important features that must be included in your calculations. However, the dimensions you mark on them must be taken from accurate measurements. You can use either metric or imperial units of measurement. Use these dimensions to calculate the actual area to be tiled. If you are unsure of this process, take the plan to your tile supplier who will be able to make the calculations for you.

For a whole room, draw up a plan like this, marking on it the dimensions of the walls, windows, doors and other features that must be considered.

For each feature, multiply the length by the height to calculate its area, adding all the resulting figures together. Subtract this figure from the total wall area to obtain the area that needs tiling.

From this, you can work out the quantity of tiles to buy, plus the amount of adhesive and grout.

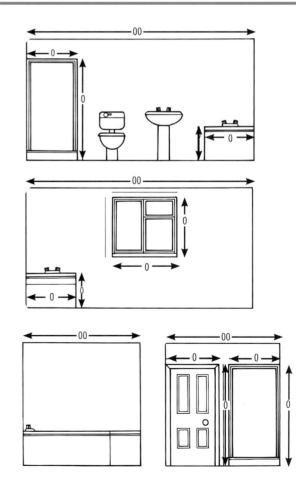

TILING PATTERNS

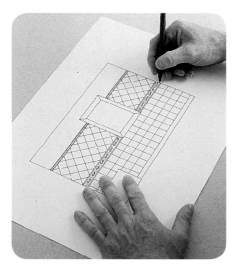

Although tiles are commonly fixed in line both horizontally and vertically, they can also be arranged in diagonal rows or in brick fashion to provide additional interest. Particularly attractive schemes can be devised by combining these arrangements in bands separated by patterned or contrasting dado tiles.

To work out the most effective pattern, use a large sheet of paper to draw up another plan of the walls, as this will allow plenty of room to fill in all the details. Having drawn in the relevant features, add the positions of patterned tiles, insets, dados, etc. Or use it to decide on the kind of tiling arrangement you would like. If you photocopy the original drawings of the walls, you can try several arrangements to see which you prefer.

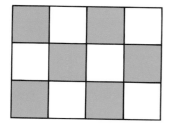

The conventional method of fixing tiles is to align the rows both horizontally and vertically, to give continuous horizontal and vertical joints.

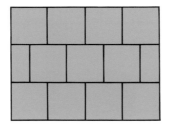

For additional interest, the tiles in each row can be staggered in relation to their neighbours, brick fashion. This works particularly well with oblong tiles.

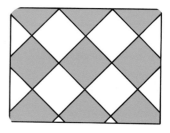

Another attractive pattern is achieved by fixing the rows of tiles diagonally to create a diamond pattern. This works best with square tiles.

COPING WITH CORNERS

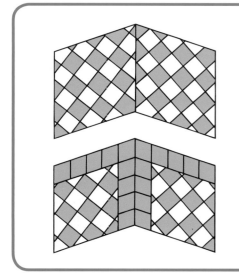

If you intend arranging the tiles in a particular pattern, or are using patterned tiles, and you are tiling adjacent walls, continuing the pattern from one wall on to another may be quite difficult (top), the more so if the corners of the room are not truly vertical. In some situations, this may be completely impossible.

A simple solution to this problem is to edge the patterned area of tiles with plain tiles fixed in conventional vertical and horizontal rows. This has the effect of producing patterned panels (bottom).

Setting out

Setting out is essential as it determines the point at which you should fix the first tile, to ensure that the overall arrangement is symmetrical.

Ideally, tile from the centre of the wall to its edges, with cut tiles at the edges at least half a tile wide. If tiling an L-shaped splashback, start with a whole tile at each end and work towards the internal corner, where any cuts should be made. If the splashback runs around three sides, tile the back wall as normal with equal cuts at each end, but work the ends back from a whole tile towards the internal corners.

TOOLS: Tape measure, pencil, spirit level, long wooden batten, gauge rod, hammer

MATERIALS: 2 50 x 25mm (2 x 1in) straight softwood battens, masonry nails

MAKING A GAUGE ROD

1 To make a gauge rod, lay out a row of tiles with tile spacers between them. Place the batten alongside, one end level with the edge of the first tile. Mark the tile positions on it, allowing for the gaps in between. With hand-made tiles, which are irregular in size, allow a spacing of 5–8mm (³⁄₁₆-⁵⁄₁₆in).

A gauge rod is an essential tool when tiling any large area, and is easily made from a wooden batten about 1.8m (6ft) long (or shorter if you are only tiling a short wall). It allows you to determine where the horizontal and vertical rows of tiles will fall on the wall, so that you can see whether tiles need to be cut at the ends of the rows. Using the rod, you can also determine the positions of the battens that will support the tiles as the tile adhesive dries (see step 9).

2 For clarity, extend the pencil marks across the face of the rod, making sure that they are square to the edge. You can do this with the aid of another tile. If you wish, you can number the divisions on the rod so that you can see at a glance how many tiles there will be in each row.

SETTING OUT

1 Measure the length of the wall to be tiled and make a pencil mark at the centre. Then, holding the straight-edged batten vertically, with the aid of a spirit level, draw a vertical line from floor to ceiling at the point of the mark.

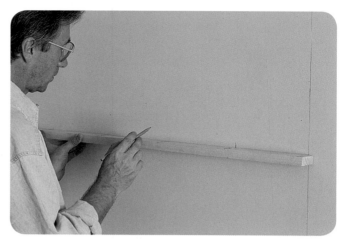

2 Hold the mark at the end of the gauge rod against the line on the wall to determine where the vertical rows of tiles will fall. On a long run, it may help to mark off the tile positions on the wall.

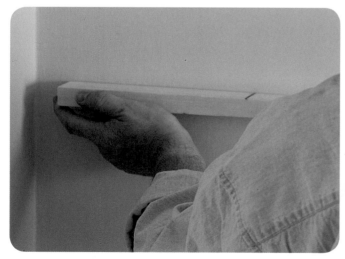

3 At the end of the wall, the gauge rod will show you whether a cut tile will be required and, if so, its width. Because you began from the centre of the wall, the same width of tile will be needed at the other end of the wall. If you are left with a very narrow gap to fill, you may have difficulty in cutting a sliver of tile to fit, and if the corner is uneven you may run into serious problems with the sliver tapering to nothing.

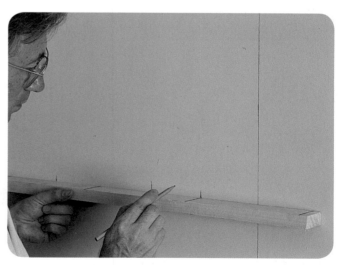

4 It will look much better if any cut tiles are at least half a tile wide. So go back to your centre line, and hold the gauge rod so that the end mark on it is offset to one side of the centre line by half a tile's width. Then make a mark on the wall in line with the end mark. Draw a new vertical line at this point, which will now be your starting point. In this way, the actual centre line of the wall will pass through the centre of a tile.

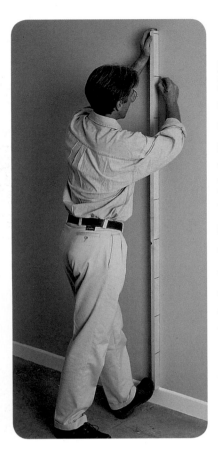

5 Next, determine the positions of the horizontal rows of tiles. First, hold the gauge rod against your vertical starting line with one end touching the skirting or floor, as appropriate. Then make a pencil mark on the wall so that it is level with the topmost mark on the gauge rod.

6 Hold the end of the rod against the ceiling and check if any mark on it aligns with the wall mark. If it does, you will not need to cut tiles for the top and bottom rows. If not, look at the gap between the wall mark and the nearest mark on the rod below it; halving this distance gives the depth of cut tiles at top and bottom. If these are very narrow, mark the wall level with the next mark down on the rod. Remember that ceilings are rarely perfectly level and often necessitate some cutting.

7 Measure the distance between the two pencil marks on the wall. Then make a third pencil mark exactly mid-way between these two points. This will give you an idea of the depth of cut tiles needed top and bottom.

8 Holding the gauge rod so that one end is just clear of the skirting, and with one of its marks aligned with the third wall mark, make another mark on the wall at the foot of the rod. This represents your starting point for the first horizontal row of tiles and ensures that the cut tiles at top and bottom will be equal in depth.

COPING WITH OBSTRUCTIONS

Windows, doors and other fixtures can complicate setting out a wall for tiling, particularly if they are towards one end of the wall. The important point to remember is to work from the centre of the most prominent visual feature when setting out, but be prepared to amend the starting point if you run into problems with very narrow cut tiles at the ends of the walls, or at windows or doors. Take your time when faced with this situation, using the gauge rod to determine the ideal starting point.

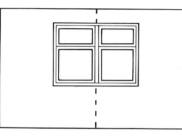

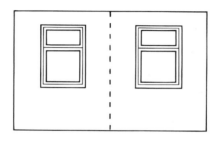

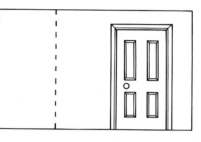

Where the wall contains a single window, placed near the centre, use the centre line of the window as your starting point when setting out with the gauge rod.

On a wall containing two windows, it is better to work from the centre line of the section of wall between the windows, as this will give a much more balanced look to the tiling.

If the door or window is offset at one end of the wall, work from the centre line of the section of wall between the furthest corner and the door or window frame.

9 Nail a horizontal wooden batten to the wall in line with the pencil mark, using a spirit level to ensure that it is perfectly level. The batten will be removed once the tile adhesive has dried and the tiles are securely fixed to the wall, so do not drive the nails all the way in.

10 When you begin tiling, work outwards from the vertical starting line. You can simply align the tiles with this line, but it will be easier with a definite edge to work from, so temporarily nail a wooden batten vertically to the wall in line with the pencil line.

3 Add the next horizontal tile and the first tile of the row above, bedding them firmly in the adhesive by wiggling them slightly while pressing firmly with your hand. Space them initially by eye.

4 Fit tile spacers to ensure even gaps for grouting. The adhesive is flexible enough to allow you to move the tiles slightly. Hand-made tiles need larger gaps, so use cardboard or offcuts of wood as spacers.

5 Carry on until you have tiled the area of adhesive. Then wipe over the faces of the tiles with a damp sponge to remove any splashes of adhesive. This is essential; if you wait until the job is finished, the adhesive will have hardened and be very difficult to remove. Carry on in this manner until all the field tiles have been stuck to the wall.

MIXING TILES

Coloured tiles or tiles with coloured patterns may vary slightly in shade from batch to batch. Using tiles from one box at a time may result in distinct colour changes across the surface. However, any variations in shade will be far less noticeable if you mix tiles from different boxes before you begin work.

Fixing uneven tiles

When tiling a wall, your aim should be to produce a perfectly flat surface, and if you have prepared the wall properly, this should not be too difficult. Any slight undulations in the wall surface can be accommodated by varying the thickness of adhesive slightly.

If the faces of the tiles are not level, the appearance of the finished job will be ruined: any light falling on the tiles will pick out high and low areas by casting tell-tale shadows. So you should check constantly for low or high tiles, and if you find any, remove them and bed them on fresh adhesive so that they match their neighbours.

TOOLS: Spirit level/wooden batten, filling knife, notched adhesive spreader, claw hammer

MATERIALS: Tile adhesive

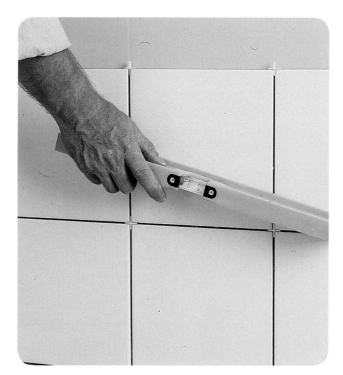

1 As you fix tiles to the wall, check from time to time that they are level by holding a straight edge, such as a spirit level or wooden batten, across them. This will show up any that are lower or higher than the rest.

2 If you find a tile that is too low or too high, lever it from the wall carefully, using a flat-bladed tool. Take care not to dislodge or damage any of the surrounding tiles, particularly if the tile being removed is in the centre of a tiled area.

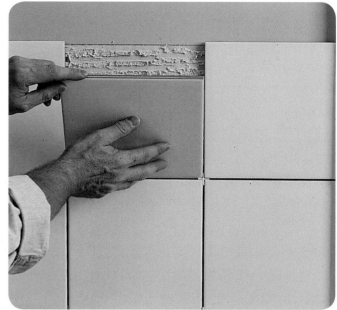

3 Scrape the adhesive from the back of the tile and spread on a fresh layer, using the notched spreader. If the tile was low, you can add a little more adhesive than normal; if high, a little less.

4 Press the tile back on to the wall, bedding it firmly and replacing any spacers to set the grouting gap. Make a final check with the straight edge that the tile is now level with its neighbours.

REMOVING THE BATTENS

1 Once you have tiled from the vertical batten to one end of the wall, you can remove the batten and work in the other direction. Then, when you have completed the wall above the horizontal batten, leave the adhesive to set before removing it. Finally, fill in between the lowest row of tiles and the skirting or floor.

Use a claw hammer to prise out the nails so that you can remove the battens. Take care not to dislodge any of the tiles that butt up against them.

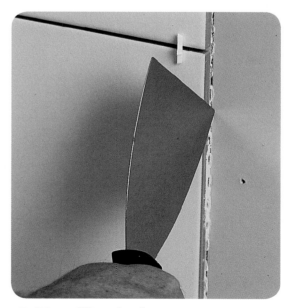

2 Use a filling knife to scrape away any adhesive that has oozed between the tiles and batten, as this may prevent you from obtaining the correct spacing between these and the subsequent tiles.

Inserting edge tiles

Unless you are extremely lucky and have a wall that is an exact number of whole tiles long and an exact number of whole tiles high, you will need to cut some tiles to fill gaps at the ends and at the top and bottom of the wall. This is not as difficult as it might first seem, and the variety of cutting tools available – if used properly – will ensure accurate cuts every time.

Accuracy is the watchword, however. Take careful measurements of the gaps that need filling, and measure for each tile that needs cutting: do not assume that all the tiles needed to fill a gap along, say, one end of a wall will be the same size, as the corners of rooms – whether between walls or between a wall and a ceiling or floor – rarely run true.

TOOLS: Tape measure, felt-tip pen/chinagraph pencil, steel rule, tile spike, tile file, notched adhesive spreader

MATERIALS: Tiles, tile adhesive, tile spacers

1 Take measurements at the top and bottom of the gap (or each end, if you are filling-in at the ceiling or floor). If the tiled area is to end at the adjacent wall, allow a gap for grouting; if the tiling is to continue on that wall, the cut tile need not fit exactly into the corner, as the tile on the adjacent wall will hide any gap.

2 Transfer the measurements to a tile with a felt-tip pen or chinagraph pencil, remembering that the cut edge is the one that should fit into the corner. Then use a steel rule and a tile spike to score the glaze between the two marks. Press firmly with the spike and score the tile once only in one smooth movement.

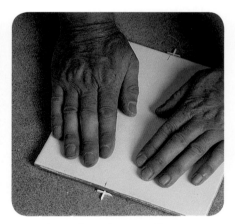

3 Place the tile on a firm surface with one leg of a tile spacer under each end of the scored line. Then press down firmly on both sides of the line and the tile should snap cleanly in two. If it does not, you probably have not scored it well enough, or the spacers may be out of line.

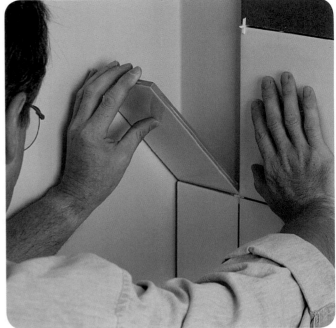

4 After cutting, clean up any roughness on the edge of the tile with a tile file, holding it at right angles to the edge.

5 Place the cut piece of tile in the gap to check whether it fits securely. If necessary, make any adjustments to its shape by filing.

6 When you are happy with the fit, spread a layer of adhesive on the back of the cut tile, using the end of the notched spreader.

7 Press the tile firmly into place, wiggling it slightly to bed it and adjusting its position so that you can insert spacers at the top and bottom.

Methods of cutting

The tile spike is the simplest and least expensive tool for cutting tiles (see page 152), and for a small job it is probably not worth investing in anything more complex. However, there are several more sophisticated tools available that make cutting tiles much easier. If you expect to be cutting a lot of tiles, or if the tiles you are using are particularly hard, it will be worth investing in one of these.

NIBBLERS

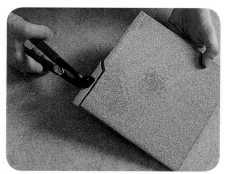

If you only have a narrow sliver to remove from a tile, or want to remove the waste from a cut-out, nibblers are essential. With these you grip a small portion of tile, then break it off by levering the tool downwards.

To remove a narrow strip from the edge of a tile, score the glaze with a tile spike. Then hold the tile firmly in one hand while gripping a portion of the waste with the nibbler jaws, close to the scored line. Lever downwards with the nibblers and a piece of waste will break away along the line. Remove the rest of the waste in the same way.

COMBINED CUTTING WHEEL/SNAPPER

This simple hand tool combines a cutting wheel for scoring the glaze of a tile with a pair of angled jaws that can be used to snap it along the scored line. It is ideal for cutting small tiles or tiles with heavily studded backs.

1 Measure the gap to be filled and mark the tile as normal. Then, using a steel rule as a guide, run the wheel over the tile between the two marks to score it. Push down firmly and score the tile only once.

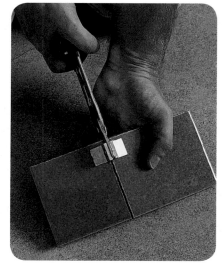

2 Place the tile in the jaws of the tool, aligning the scored line carefully with the centre of the angled jaws. Squeeze the handles together and the tile will snap cleanly along the scored line; surprisingly little pressure is required. Be careful not to let the pieces drop, as they may shatter if they hit a hard surface.

TILE-CUTTING MACHINE

If you expect to be cutting a lot of tiles, particularly if they are large and/or very hard, it will be worth investing in a tile-cutting machine. Alternatively, you should be able to hire one from a tool hire shop. Several different types of machine are available, some offering more facilities than others. All, however, combine a scoring function with a snapping action that requires very little pressure.

1 Some machines are provided with a removable gauge that allows you to measure the gap to be filled. This particular version makes an allowance for the grouting gap. Fit it so that the end of the gauge is resting firmly against the adjacent wall or tiled surface, and the tabs of the sliding portion against the edge of the neighbouring tile. A simple over-centre lever can then be used to lock the gauge in this position, allowing it to be transferred to the machine.

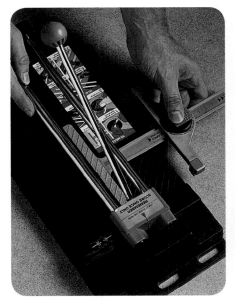

2 Having locked the sliding portion of the gauge in place, fit the assembly into its cut-out in the bed of the machine. Take care not to disturb the gauge setting while you are doing this, otherwise the tile will be cut to the incorrect size.

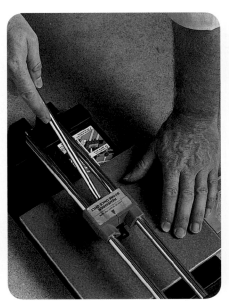

3 Place the tile in the machine, aligning one edge with the tabs of the gauge and the other with the stops moulded into the bed. Bring the scriber into contact with the tile, press down firmly and push the handle forwards to score the glaze.

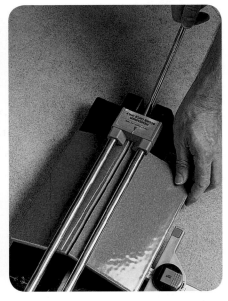

4 Set the tile under the handle slide so that the scored line on the tile is aligned with the mark on the slide. Then lower the handle to bring the snapper into contact with the underside of the tile. Press down and the tile will snap in two.

Grouting

Once you have fixed all the tiles to the wall, the adhesive should be allowed to dry before the gaps between the tiles are grouted. The amount of time for the adhesive to dry will vary depending on the type of adhesive used: see the manufacturer's instructions.

Some grouts are supplied in powder form for mixing with water, while others come ready-mixed. Make sure you have sufficient to complete the tiled area, and be prepared to work quickly, as it will begin to harden and become unworkable quite quickly. Use a waterproof version for a shower cubicle. Before applying the grout, either remove the tile spacers or push them in as far as they will go.

TOOLS: Small trowel, grout spreader/squeegee, grout shaper, sponge, bucket, soft clean cloth

MATERIALS: Grout, water

1 Use the trowel to scoop up some grout and press it on to the face of the tiles. Then spread the grout with the squeegee, wiping it from the face of the tiles and pressing it into the open joints between them. Use a smooth, diagonal, sweeping action, working up and across the tiles. Work quickly until you have grouted all the joints.

2 Carefully go over the tiled area with a damp sponge to remove all traces of grout from the surface of the tiles. Do this as soon as you finish applying the grout, as it will be very difficult to remove once it has been allowed to harden. Take care not to drag any grout from the joints while you are doing this.

GROUT SHAPERS

You can either buy a special tool for shaping grout or make your own. Some ready-made grout shapers offer a choice of profile size and have interchangeable heads so that when one becomes worn, another can be fitted.

Alternatively, you can use a large-diameter wooden dowel with the end neatly and smoothly rounded off, or even the tip of an old plastic paintbrush handle. If you do choose either of these home-made tools, experiment on a small area of tiling first in case the material discolours the grout.

1 This proprietary grout shaper features four interchangeable sections that offer a choice of shaping profiles. They also allow a fresh profile to be selected when the one in use becomes worn.

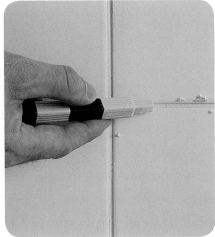

2 Shape the grout after it has hardened slightly, holding the tool so that it runs along the edges of the adjacent tiles, the corner of the tip smoothing the grout. Sponge off excess grout.

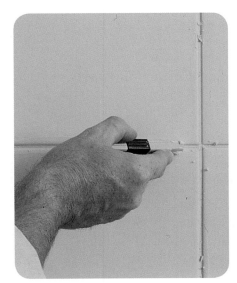

3 Allow the grout to harden slightly, then shape the joints to give a uniform appearance. Pull the shaper along each vertical and horizontal joint in one continuous movement. Remove any surplus grout with a sponge.

4 If the shaping process exposes any gaps or holes in the grouted joints, press a small amount of fresh grout into them with your fingertip. Then shape the joint as before and remove any surplus.

5 Leave the grout to harden fully. As the sponged face of the tiles dries, you will notice a powdery residue covering the surface. This should be polished off with a soft, clean cloth to leave a perfect finish.

Dados and borders

If you are tiling a small area, you may want to edge it with a decorative border. Indeed, you may have no option if the tiles you are using do not have glazed edges. Standard-sized tiles can be used for borders, but they tend to dominate the rest of the tiled area. Proprietary border tiles, which are much narrower than standard tiles, are a better choice.

A dado, which runs along the wall at waist height, is a useful means of breaking up a large expanse of tiles. As with borders, contrasting or patterned standard tiles can be used to form a dado. However, purpose-made dado tiles offer the greatest flexibility in terms of width, colour and pattern.

Dado and border tiles may not match the size of your field tiles. If this is the case, their joints should be staggered in relation to the joints between the field tiles.

TOOLS: Tape measure, felt-tip pen/chinagraph pencil, steel rule, tile saw, a small trowel, notched adhesive spreader, sponge, bucket, tile spike, tile file

MATERIALS: Border or dado tiles, tile adhesive, tile spacers, water

CUTTING MOULDED DADO TILES

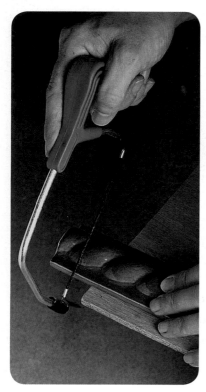

Dado tiles with a moulded relief pattern are impossible to score and snap in the normal way when cutting them to length. The solution is to cut them with a tile saw. Mark the tile for length with a felt-tip pen or chinagraph pencil, then cut along the line with the tile saw.

TILING A SMALL AREA

The principle of tiling a small area, such as a splashback behind a washbasin, is the same as a large area (see page 148), except that it is always made up of whole tiles. For this reason, small tiles are the best choice.

Depending on the size of the tiles, you can make a small splashback by tiling up to the edges of the basin only. Alternatively, you can move the starting point by half a tile to one side of the basin's centre point, so that it projects beyond the basin at each side of the basin.

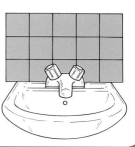

CORNER TILES

When fixing border tiles, you may find that you need to change the direction of the tiles from horizontal to vertical. If the tiles are a plain colour, there will be no problems; you can simply overlap the end of one tile with another. However, if they are patterned, this method will not produce a very neat corner, as the pattern will not match. Fortunately, there are two possible solutions.

1 Depending on the pattern, it may be possible to mitre the ends of the adjacent tiles so that the design continues around the corner without an apparent break. You may need to trim the tiles carefully to obtain a good match. Cut both before fixing them to the wall.

2 When the tiles have been grouted, the mitred joint will look neat and unobtrusive. Note how the joints of the border tiles have been staggered in relation to those of the field tiles. This is necessary because of the difference in their sizes.

3 In some cases, the pattern may be impossible to match up by mitring the ends of the tiles. In this situation, the answer is to fill the corner with a small square of plain tile, which can be cut easily from a larger one.

4 Here the square of tile has been cut from one of the coloured field tiles, but a plain white tile would have worked as well. Make sure you use a tile with glazed edges, cutting the square from a corner to provide two glazed sides.

Corners

The most common problem when tiling walls is dealing with corners. You may have to cope with an external corner (one that projects outwards), an internal corner, or both; a different method is used in each case to ensure a neat finish.

The important consideration is that the horizontal rows of tiles on the adjacent surfaces must align. You must take care when setting out to ensure that the support battens are perfectly aligned with each other, as any misalignment will be immediately noticeable and will spoil the finished tiling. Check with a spirit level that an external angle is truly vertical. If it is not, the ends of the tiles will need to overlap it slightly, tile trim being used to finish off the corner neatly.

TOOLS: Tape measure, pencil, spirit level, hacksaw, small trowel, notched adhesive spreader, sponge, bucket

MATERIALS: Tiles, tile adhesive, corner trim, tile spacers, water

INTERNAL CORNERS

At an internal corner, the tiles on one wall are fixed so that they overlap the ends of the tiles on the adjacent wall. The result should be a neat grouted joint in the angle between the two walls.

You will probably have to cut tiles to fit into the corner on both walls, but if you can fix uncut tiles on one wall, for neatness use them to conceal the cut edges of the others.

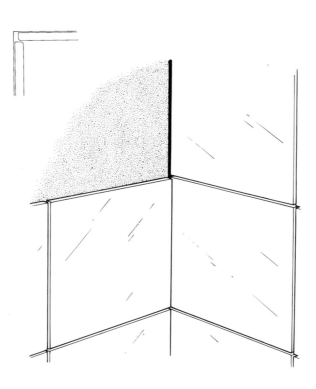

Tile one wall completely first, cutting the edge tiles into the angle between the two walls. They do not have to be an exact fit since the overlapping tiles will hide any slight gap between them and the facing wall. When tiling the neighbouring wall, take accurate measurements for each edge tile, allowing for the grouting between it and the existing tiled wall. Then fix the tiles in place to complete the corner.

EXTERNAL CORNERS

At an external corner, the simplest solution is to use plastic corner trim to hide the edges of the tiles and provide a neat finish to the angle between the adjacent walls. The trim has a quadrant profile with a perforated mounting flange for bedding in the tile adhesive. They are available in a range of colours, to suit different thicknesses of tile.

1 Tile one of the walls completely, so that the edges of the tiles are flush with the end of the wall. Cut the corner trim to length with a hacksaw, then apply a narrow band of tile adhesive to the face of the other wall (called the return wall) from top to bottom. Carefully press the trim into the adhesive, aligning it with the edges of the tiles on the adjacent wall. Remember to insert tile spacers between the trim and edges of the tiles.

2 Spread more adhesive on the second (return) wall, working the spreader vertically, rather than horizontally. This will prevent the spreader from catching the trim and pulling it from the corner.

3 Tile the return wall, working away from the corner trim. Place the tiles so that they almost touch the trim, then fit tile spacers between the trim and the tiles to ensure an even grouted joint. Grout the joints as normal when the adhesive has set.

GLAZED-EDGE TILES

If you are using tiles with bevelled or rounded glazed edges, you can tackle external corners without the need for corner trim, provided the corner is truly vertical. Simply fix the tiles on one wall so that they overlap the edges of the tiles on the other.
 Tile the return wall so that the tiles are flush with the face of the main wall. Then fix the glazed-edge tiles on the main wall so that they overlap and conceal the edges of the tiles on the return wall.

Recessed windows

Tiling a window recess produces it own particular problems, as it has effectively an external corner all the way round, requiring the corner trim to be joined at the ends. In addition, the reveal is likely to be quite narrow and will involve cutting tiles to fit in. You will also need to find some means of holding tiles in place at the top of the recess while the adhesive sets.

The procedure is to tile the face of the wall surrounding the window recess first, then the underside of the reveal, the sides, and finally the bottom.

TOOLS: Tape measure, pencil, small trowel, notched adhesive spreader, tile spike, steel rule, hacksaw, hammer

MATERIALS: Tiles, tile adhesive, corner trim, wooden battens, masonry nails

1 Begin by tiling the face of the wall up to the window recess so that the edges of the tiles are flush with the recess. Cut lengths of corner trim to fit around the recess, mitring the ends so that they fit neatly together.

2 To mitre the ends of the corner trim, measure back along one side a distance equal to its width. Join this point with the opposite corner and saw off the piece of waste. Fit spacers when fixing the trim.

3 When tiling the recess itself, fix whole tiles around the outer edge of the recess so that they butt up to the corner trim. Then fill in the remaining space against the window frame with cut tiles.

SUPPORTING THE TILES

The main problem when tiling a window recess completely is holding the tiles in place at the top of the recess while the adhesive sets. This applies to both the tiles on the face of the wall and on the underside of the recess. The simplest method is to use wooden battens for temporary support while the tile and adhesive sets.

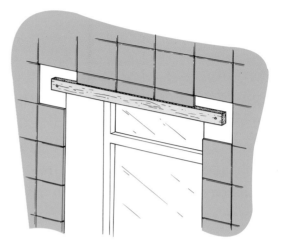

▲ To support the tiles on the face of the wall, temporarily nail a wooden batten in place so that its upper edge is level with the underside of the recess. When the tiles have been fixed in place and the adhesive has set completely, remove the batten and finish tiling the face of the wall where the batten was nailed.

◄ To support the tiles on the underside of the recess while the adhesive sets, use a wooden batten wedged in place with two uprights.

OVERLAPPING EDGES

Tiles with glazed edges can be used to finish around a window recess without the need for corner trim, as with external corners. One set of tiles – those on the horizontal window sill – simply overlap the edges of those on the adjacent vertical surface.

As with corner trim, fix tiles to the face of the wall so that their top edges are flush with the recess. Then fix whole tiles in place around the recess so that they overlap the edges of the tiles on the face of the wall.

Pipes

Some rooms that need tiling have pipes that either pass through the wall or run along its face. Ideally, these should be concealed by boxing them in. If, however, boxing is not feasible, you may have to cut a tile to fit around a pipe, or drill the face of the tiles for pipe clips. Neither task is particularly difficult, but when cutting around a pipe, you must measure and mark out your tile with care if it is to fit accurately.

You can use the same technique for tiling around an electrical outlet or switch, but for this, turn off the power to the circuit, remove the faceplate, tile up to the edge of the box behind, then replace the faceplate.

TOOLS: Pencil, felt-tip pen/chinagraph pencil, steel rule, tile spike, narrow nibblers, tile file, hammer, electric drill, masonry/tile bit, screwdriver

MATERIALS: Tiles, tile adhesive, pipe offcut, masking tape, masonry nail, wall plugs, screws, pipe clips

CUTTING AROUND A PIPE

If only one tile will be affected when cutting around a pipe, the technique is to split the tile on the centre line of the pipe and make a semicircular cut-out in each piece to fit around the pipe. If the position of the pipe coincides with a joint between tiles, this procedure will have to be adapted to suit.

2 Next, transfer the pencil marks to the tile that will be cut around the pipe, using a felt-tip pen or chinagraph pencil. Remember to place tile spacers in position so that the marks will be in the correct position on the tile.

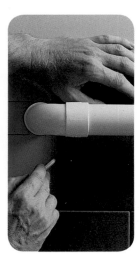

1 Having tiled the wall to one side and below the pipe, use a tile and a pencil to mark lines on the wall level with the top, bottom and sides of the pipe where it projects from the wall.

3 Using another tile as a guide to ensure that the lines are at right angles to the edges of the tile, extend the marks across the face with your felt-tip pen or chinagraph pencil. Where the pairs of lines intersect, carefully draw around an offcut of pipe of the correct diameter to mark out the area to be removed.

PIPE CLIPS

If you want to run a pipe across the face of a tiled surface, you will have to drill the tiles for fixing screws and fit pipe clips. The same technique can be used for fixing any surface-mounted fitting, such as a mirror or soap dish, to a tiled surface.

1 Cover the area of the tile to be drilled with masking tape. This will allow you to mark the hole positions with a pencil and will help prevent the drill bit from skidding. To ensure accuracy when drilling, break the glaze at the point to be drilled by lightly tapping on a masonry nail with a hammer. Drill holes for the screws, using a bit that matches the size of the wall plugs to be used.

2 Having drilled the holes to the correct depth, remove the masking tape from the face of the tile and fit plastic wall plugs in the holes. Finally, offer up the pipe and clip, securing the latter to the wall by driving the screws into the plastic plugs.

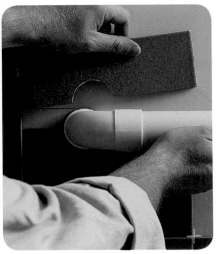

4 Score across the face of the tile so that the scored line passes through the centre of the circle. Whether you score the line vertically or horizontally will depend on the way the pipe runs; use the pipe itself to conceal as much of the cut as possible. Then snap the tile in two.

5 Using narrow nibblers, carefully remove the waste from within each semicircle. When you get close to the line, offer up the tile to check its fit. Having removed enough waste, carefully smooth the edges with a tile file. Then clean the face of the tile to remove the pen marks.

6 Make a final check before fixing the pieces of tile to the wall. Then spread adhesive on them and stick them in place. If you scored the tile correctly, the joint between the two pieces should be almost invisible. Fill any slight gap around the pipe when you grout the tiles.

Bathroom fittings

There may be occasions when you need to tile around an item with a large, irregular shape, such as a washbasin or a similar fitting in a bathroom. In this situation, the ideal solution is to pull the item away from the wall as much as possible and tile behind it, even if this involves modifying any pipework slightly: the end result will certainly be much neater. If this is not possible, you will need to make cut-outs in the tiles surrounding the item so that they fit neatly against it.

TOOLS: Scissors, felt-tip pen/chinagraph pencil, tile spike, steel rule, nibblers, tile file, profile gauge, spirit level, tape measure

MATERIALS: Tiles, paper, self-adhesive tape

IDEAL TOOLS

Tile saw

Although nibblers can be used to make cut-outs in tiles, you may find that a tile saw is easier to use. This looks like a small hacksaw, but it has a special blade that will cut through ceramic tiles with ease. Having marked the area to be cut out of the tile, hold it firmly and simply saw along the outline. Because the blade is round, you can change direction quite easily and cut quite tight curves.

Profile gauge

A profile gauge is useful for transferring an unusual shape to a tile. It incorporates a large number of sliding plastic 'needles' which duplicate the shape of an item as the tool is pushed against it. The gauge is ideal for use with small tiles, but for larger tiles you may have to find some way of supporting it in the correct position to cover the required area of the tile.

1 The simplest method for transferring the shape of the basin to the tile is to make a paper template. First, cut a piece of paper to the size of the tile, then make scissor cuts in the paper so that you have a series of paper 'fingers'. The direction in which you make the cuts will depend on the position of the cut-out. In this case, the shape will be in the corner of the tile, so cuts are made in both directions.

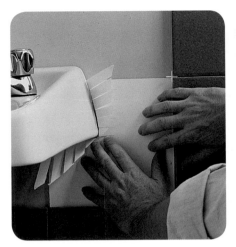

2 With tile spacers in place between the adjacent tiles, hold the paper in position as if it was a tile. Smooth the paper against the wall and fold the paper fingers back where they meet the basin.

3 Tape the fingers down to prevent them from moving about, then lay the paper template on top of the tile to be cut. Mark the outline of the cut-out on the tile with a felt-tip pen or chinagraph pencil.

4 In this case, a large portion of the waste can be removed by simply scoring a line diagonally across it with a tile spike, then snapping it off with a pair of nibblers. This will save you time.

5 The remaining waste must be removed with nibblers. Do not try to snap off too much at once; take your time and break off small pieces, working towards the outline. As you get close to the line, take even smaller 'bites', until eventually you are almost scraping off slivers of tile.

6 Smooth the edge of the tile with a tile file, then hold the tile against the wall to check the fit around the basin. If necessary, adjust the fit with the nibblers and tile file. When you are happy that you have a uniform gap around the basin, you can fix the tile to the wall.

7 Continue to cut and fit tiles around the rest of the washbasin in the same manner. When you have finished, you can tile the remainder of the wall as normal. The gap around the washbasin should be grouted when you grout the tiles to leave a neat finish.

Waterproof seals

When tiling behind a sink, basin or bath, it is important to ensure a watertight seal along the bottom of the tiled area, to prevent any water from seeping through the joint.

In most cases, a bead of silicone sealant run along the joint will be sufficient. Silicone sealants, available in white and a limited range of colours, are sold in syringe-like dispensers containing enough to run a bead around the average size of bath. Larger tubes suitable for use with a metal, trigger-type dispenser are also available.

Alternatively, use quadrant tiles or plastic sealing strip. Though the latter gives a neater finish, both are useful for sealing a gap between a tiled splashback and a bath.

TOOLS: Sealant dispenser, hacksaw, tile saw, small trowel, notched adhesive spreader, grout spread sponge, clean cloth, bucket

MATERIALS: Silicone sealant/plastic sealing strip/quadrant tiles, tile adhesive, tile spacers, grout, tissue paper

SILICONE SEALANT

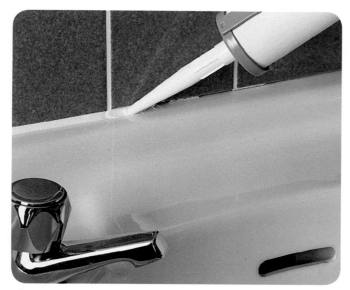

If using a trigger dispenser, place the nozzle of the sealant tube at one end of the splashback and apply a smooth bead along its length, squeezing the trigger steadily as you do so. You can smooth any slight irregularities with a finger moistened with water, but take care, as you may ruin the appearance and, worse, the waterproof seal.

QUADRANT TILES

Quadrant tiles have a curved profile that directs water back away from a tiled surface. Before fitting them it is worth sealing the gap between the bath and the wall with silicone sealant. Then fix the tiles with adhesive, pressing them firmly into place. Use tile spacers to space the tiles while the adhesive sets. Grout all tiles in the normal way.

PLASTIC SEALING STRIP

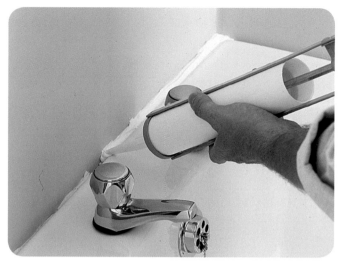

1 Sometimes there is a tapered gap between one side of a fitting, particularly baths, and the wall. A very slight deviation could well be hidden by the thickness of the tiles and adhesive, but any significant amount will need concealing with a proprietary sealing strip.

2 Before you add the sealing strip and tiles, fill the gap with silicone sealant. If the gap is quite wide, wedge in some crumpled tissue paper to act as a support for the sealant. Apply a good bead of sealant, adding extra in the corner where the ends of the sealing strip will meet.

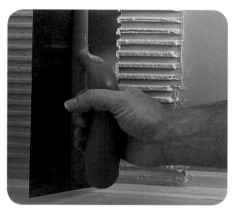

4 Having set out the splashback and decided on a starting point, spread a layer of adhesive on the wall. Work on a small area at a time to ensure that the adhesive remains workable. Make sure it overlaps the sealing strip completely.

3 Some sealing strips have a self-adhesive backing. Simply peel off the protective paper and press the strip against the wall so that its flexible blade makes a good seal with the top of the bath. Mitre the ends where they meet in the corner, adding more silicone if necessary to ensure a watertight joint. If the strip has no self-adhesive backing, bed it in tile adhesive.

5 Add the tiles, cutting the edge tiles as required (see pages 152–153). Make sure the tiles are bedded properly, and add spacers to ensure uniform grout gaps. Grout the tiles in the normal manner.

Renovation and repair

In time, grout can become discoloured and stained. Though using a proprietary grout cleaner can often solve the problem, it will sometimes be necessary to rake out all of the old grout and replace it with fresh. Doing this will make even an old tiled surface look like new.

Similarly, damaged tiles or tiles with unsightly screw holes that cannot be filled can be replaced. In a tiled splashback, such damage will allow water to seep through to the wall behind with potentially disastrous results. In a kitchen, cracked or broken tiles can harbour dirt and germs and should be replaced.

TOOLS: Grout raker, small trowel, grout spreader, sponge, grout shaper, clean cloth, bucket, electric drill, ceramic tile/masonry bit, cold chisel, hammer, thick gloves, goggles, small trowel, notched adhesive spreader, wooden batten

MATERIALS: Tile adhesive, tile spacers, grout, water

RENEWING GROUT

1 Use a proper grout raker to remove the old grout from around the tiles, taking care not to damage their edges. Do all the vertical joints, then the horizontal joints, or vice versa, so that you don't miss any. Make sure you remove the grout down to at least half the thickness of the tile.

2 Apply fresh grout to the tiled surface (see page 156). Use a wet sponge to clean off excess grout from the face of the tiles. When the grout has hardened slightly, run a grout shaper along the joints (see page 157). Once the grout is dry, polish the face of the tiles with a soft, clean cloth.

GROUT RAKERS

Grout is designed to provide a hard filling for the joints between tiles and so requires a sharp, pointed tool to scrape it out.

The toothed grout raker on the left has a thin blade suitable for narrow joints, while the tool on the right will cope with wider joints. The latter can also be used for scoring tiles prior to cutting.

REPLACING A DAMAGED TILE

1 In this case, a tile is being replaced after a wall-mounted fitting has been removed, exposing two unsightly screw holes. The first job is to rake out the grout completely on all four sides of the tile.

2 Drill a series of holes around the centre of the tile, using a ceramic tile bit and an electric drill. Since the tile is being removed, even a masonry bit can be used without tape, as if it slips slightly it will not matter.

IDEAL TOOL
A ceramic tile drill bit is designed to bite immediately into the glaze of a tile without skidding, removing the need for masking tape or breaking through the glaze with a sharp pointed tool. Various sizes of bit are available to suit a range of hole diameters.

3 Use a hammer and cold chisel to cut through the tile between the holes and chop out the central portion of the tile. Wear gloves to protect your hands and goggles to shield your eyes from flying fragments, which can be sharp.

4 Work towards the edges of the tile, gently breaking pieces away. Be very careful when you get close to the neighbouring tiles. With the tile removed, chisel out as much adhesive as possible; when you insert a dry tile it must not stand proud.

5 Then coat the back of the tile with adhesive and set it in place. Use a wooden batten to ensure that it is flush with the adjacent tiles and fit tile spacers to ensure uniform grout joints. Grout the tile in the usual manner (see page 156).

CHAPTER 4

PAINTING EXTERIORS

When you paint the exterior of your home, you are doing more than simply decorating it. You are also protecting and preserving it from all aspects of the weather. Keeping exterior walls, wood and metal-work in a sound condition is necessary to avoid damage that may affect the interior of your home.

Exterior decorating projects are usually on a large scale, so it is vital to plan the work correctly. By using the right materials and equipment and following a logical order of work, you will reduce both the time and effort needed to complete the job.

This chapter explains the correct way to prepare masonry, woodwork and metal surfaces, and then goes on to explain step-by-step the correct way to tackle the task of painting, ensuring that the result looks good and protects your home for as long as possible.

Painting masonry

Clearly, walls are the largest surfaces on a house and are therefore the most dominant aspect in the overall appearance of your home. When it comes to choosing colours or finishes there are general guidelines that may be observed. Pale colours appear to expand surface areas whereas darker colours tend to contract them. Darker colours do not show the dirt readily but lighter colours tend to produce a more reflective, brighter appearance.

Before making final decisions and purchasing the full quantity of paint, try some test areas. Experiment both in sunlight and shade. Be sure to consider what other colours or finishes are being used on windows and doors, and whether the selections will complement each other.

◄ Smooth render, painted white, is a safe but extremely practical use of colour for highlighting other features and providing a perfect backdrop for plants and garden accessories. Selective use in a courtyard or patio area, for example, will immediately brighten up dark, dingy corners, giving a light, airy feel and impression of space.

► Textured coatings or paint are practical, hard-wearing finishes. They also add depth to wall surfaces and contrast well with other masonry surfaces.

▼ When choosing colours it is often necessary to try and complement other aspects of the property, such as the garden, architectural features that need highlighting, or in this case, blending the smooth render colour with natural stone.

▲ The use of colour on masonry also helps to match up two different surfaces. Some houses often look slightly disjointed if they combine too many types of masonry. Therefore blending the two together can help form a more complete and harmonious effect.

Exterior paint finishes

Almost all paints suitable for the exterior of houses can be divided into two broad categories: water-based and solvent-based (see page 29 for a comparison of the two).

Water-based paints are becoming increasingly popular, mainly because they are easy to use and are environmentally friendly. The more traditional solvent-based paints are less user friendly than their water-based counterparts.

GUIDE TO PAINT FINISHES

	PRODUCT DESCRIPTION	SUITABLE SURFACES	MAIN QUALITIES	LIMITATIONS	APPLICATION METHOD
PRIMER	Watery, dilute appearance specifically formulated to seal bare surfaces.	Use stabilising primer for masonry. All purpose primers are available.	Good sealer enabling application of further coats of paint. Many have preservative qualities.	Only use is on bare or unstable surfaces.	Brush.
PRIMER-UNDERCOAT	A primer and undercoat in one, providing base for top coat(s).	Bare wood.	Easy to use, time-saving, quick drying.	Only available water-based.	Brush, roller, conventional or airless spray.
UNDERCOAT	Dull, opaque finish providing ideal base for application of top coat(s).	Any primed surface.	Hard-wearing.	Lengthier application procedure compared to primer undercoat.	Brush or roller.
SMOOTH MASONRY PAINT	Flat matt or mid sheen finishing paint. Majority are water based.	Most masonry surfaces.	Hard-wearing, most contain fungicide. Spreads further than textured counterparts.	Shows surface imperfections more clearly than textured equivalents.	Brush, roller conventional or airless spray.
TEXTURED MASONRY PAINT	Textured, 'gritty' matt or mid sheen finishing paint. Majority are water-based.	Most masonry surfaces.	Hides surface imperfections, most contain fungicide.	Poor spreading capacity compared to smooth masonry paint.	Brush, roller or conventional spray.
TEXTURED FINISHING COATING	Highly textured, thick, paint coating.	Most masonry surfaces.	Extremely hard-wearing, flexible, hides cracks and surface imperfections.	Very low spreading capacity and therefore expensive to use.	Trowel/Float, roller, or conventional spray.
GLOSS	Polished, shiny finishing paint.	Any undercoated surface, ideally wood or metal.	Very hard-wearing decorative finish. Easy to clean.	Application takes longer than most other paints, and requires a sound technique.	Brush or roller.
METAL FINISHING PAINT	Mid sheen or gloss, available in a number of smooth or textured finishes.	Any bare or previously painted metal surfaces, excluding aluminium.	Hard-wearing, prevents rust.	Poor finish on large surface areas.	Brush, roller or aerosol.

GUIDE TO NATURAL WOOD FINISHES

	PRODUCT DESCRIPTION	SUITABLE SURFACES	MAIN QUALITIES	LIMITATIONS	APPLICATION METHOD
VARNISH	Translucent natural wood finish available in gloss, semi-gloss or matt, totally sealing surface.	All bare wood. Darker colours may be applied over previously stained surfaces.	Highly decorative and easy to clean, some contain fungicide.	Not very durable.	Brush.
STAIN	Deep penetrating natural wood finish. Variety of sheens available.	All bare wood, although hardwoods produce the best finishes.	Hard-wearing. Enhances the grain and features of natural wood.	Difficult to strip or change colour once applied, so care is needed in initial choices.	Brush.
OIL	Penetrating natural wood treatment.	All bare or previously preserved wood.	Can be used mainly as a nourishing preservative or provide a polished finish.	Regular applications required. Care needed when disposing of cloths.	Brush and/or cloth. Cloth for removing surplus.

ORDER OF WORK

Masonry paint on new render
1 Bare render
2 First coat of masonry paint
3 Second coat of masonry paint

Masonry paint on old render
1 Old, painted masonry surface
2 Fungicide
3 Stabilising solution/primer
4 First coat of masonry paint
5 Second coat of masonry paint

Oil-based paint on bare wood
1 Bare wood
2 Knotter on bare wood knots
3 Primer (pink) or preservative primer (green)
4 Undercoat: two coats recommended
5 Gloss

Water-based paint on wood
1 Bare wood
2 Knotter on bare wood knots
3 Primer-undercoat
4 Gloss: two coats recommended

Wood stain
1 Bare wood
2 Preservative base coat (solvent-based systems only)
3 First coat of stain
4 Second coat of stain. (Third coat may be required for water-based systems)

Varnish
1 Bare wood
2 Preservative base coat
3 First coat of varnish
4 Second coat of varnish

Ladder safety

Painting the exterior of a house will almost inevitably involve work up a ladder, therefore it is important to know how to position a ladder correctly and to be aware of all the safety rules. Aluminium and other lightweight ladders are lighter, more durable and therefore easier to use than traditional wooden ladders. For all-purpose use the best buy is an extension ladder which consists of two ladders that can be used separately or joined together to gain access to high areas around the home.

TOOLS: Ladder, hammer, ladder stand-off, roofing attachment

MATERIALS: Pads of cloth, masking tape, wooden board, batten, rope, wooden stakes

POSITIONING A LADDER

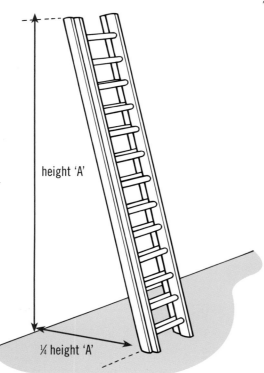

height 'A'

¼ height 'A'

To raise a ladder to an upright position, place it flat on the ground with the bottom feet of the ladder at the base of a wall. Go to the other end of the ladder, pick up the top rung and hold it above your head. Moving hand over hand gradually 'walk' the ladder up into a position where it is vertical against the wall. Now move the bottom feet out into a position where the distance from the base of the ladder to the bottom of the wall is one quarter of the distance from the bottom of the wall to the top of the ladder. At whatever height you use the ladder, always maintain this angle.

SAFETY CHECKLIST

1 Position the ladder correctly, taking extra care on uneven ground.
2 Never over-reach: get down and move the ladder to a new position.
3 Never go up a ladder higher than having the top rung at waist height.
4 Never rest a ladder on guttering or downpipes.
5 Never leave a ladder unattended.
6 Always try to keep one hand on the ladder.
7 Regularly check the ladder – especially a wooden one – for any damage or wear.
8 Never rush when climbing up a ladder.

WALL PROTECTION

To protect wall surfaces from being scraped during painting, bind the top two stays of the ladder with pads of cloth held securely in place with masking tape.

SOFT GROUND

Most modern ladders have rubber feet which prevent any movement on hard surfaces. On uneven or soft ground, place the base of the ladder on a board. A batten, attached to the back of the board, will reduce the risk of movement.

EXTRA STABILITY

If the ground you are working on is soft and spongy, take the extra precaution of roping one of the bottom rungs of the ladder on to two stakes hammered securely into the ground.

USEFUL ATTACHMENTS

Ladder stand-off

This will make it considerably easier to work on protruding fascia or barge boards. Stand-offs are clipped on to the top two to three rungs, thus bringing the top of the ladder away from the wall.

Roofing ladder attachments

These can be bolted on to most modern ladders. They enable you to reach dormer windows on a pitched roof. The roofing attachment hooks over the ridge of the roof so you are able to climb up the ladder with no fear of it slipping.

Clearing the way

Before any work can begin it is essential to remove any obstacles that restrict access to outside walls. Plants and shrubs need consideration as there is nothing more irritating than trying to hold a stray branch away from an area you are painting, and in fact this would be dangerous to attempt while up a ladder.

TOOLS: Ladder, secateurs, dust sheet, spade, screwdriver, bucket, plier wrench

1 Use a pair of secateurs or garden shears to trim back creepers and shrubs. This is especially important around guttering as overgrown vegetation will quickly block gutters, causing joints to leak. Such leaks will cause water damage to decorating which has been carried out on the walls, or even windows, below.

2 If possible, remove guttering to allow easy access to fascia boards. Plastic guttering will normally unclip easily; a slot-headed screwdriver is often useful to gently lever the clips holding up the guttering. Other guttering, such as metal, is often more difficult to take down and may need to be painted in position (see pages 198–199).

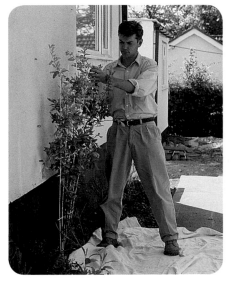

ELECTRICAL SAFETY
The mains electricity supply enters many houses through cables located at a high level. Extra caution needs to be taken when working close to such a hazard, especially when a ladder is being used. Contact your local electricity board to find out its recommended safety procedure and whether it needs to bind the cables with non-conductive sleeves before starting any repair or painting work to avoid any risk of electric shock.

3 Shrubs and plants on trellises up against walls are common obstacles. Wherever possible, unfasten any supporting wires or screws and gently pull the trellis or shrub forward, away from the wall, on to a dust sheet.

4 To reduce the risk of damaging a plant, use a bucket to support its weight. Make sure that everything is covered with a dust sheet, as this prevents any contamination by overspray when you start to paint.

5 Where there is no clear dividing line between the wall and the level of the ground, use a spade to pull back 5–10cm (2–4in) of soil or gravel away from the base of the wall. By doing this you will avoid getting dirt or grit in the paintbrush when painting at this low level and it will ensure a neat finish at ground level when the soil is replaced, after painting has been completed.

6 Removable metal-work, such as hanging basket brackets or light fittings, should also be taken down at this stage. This speeds up the painting process by giving an obstacle-free wall and also allows you to paint such items with greater ease (see pages 198–199).

Types of masonry

When planning to paint a bare masonry wall, you need to consider whether it is, in fact, suitable for a painted finish. Some surfaces accept paint better than others, and some types of masonry finish would be completely spoiled by the application of paint.

Outlined below are some of the more common types of masonry that you may have on your house.

RENDER

New render should be allowed to dry out thoroughly before it is painted. It then provides a perfect surface for painting. Rendered finishes vary a great deal, ranging from very smooth to rough cast.

TEXTURED FINISHES

Most textured finishes are self coloured and have been applied by a trowel and/or a roller. However, they may be over-painted successfully once they are discoloured or shabby from general wear and tear.

TYROLEAN

This is a different type of textured finish that is splattered on to the wall using a special hand-held machine. It is self coloured but, like other textured finishes, can be successfully overpainted if desired.

BRICKS

Common house bricks may be painted, but poor paint adhesion can sometimes be a problem. In particular, bricks that have been given a glazed finish should not be painted over.

BREEZE BLOCKS

Normally used for internal wall blockwork, but are often found used for small exterior retaining walls. Paint application is difficult because they have a porous surface that is full of tiny holes.

NATURAL STONE

There are many different types of stone, but they are not normally painted, as they have a natural beauty already. Also, painting can be difficult because the surface starts to flake and crumble.

RECONSTRUCTED STONE

Many different varieties, all of which are made from crushed stone moulded into easy-to-use building blocks. Their natural attractiveness reduces the need for painting, but they will accept paint if required.

Identifying exterior problems

Exterior wall surfaces are constantly under attack from the elements. As well as temperature changes and the destructive properties of water in its various forms, general wear and tear and poor decoration in the past all contribute to the breakdown of a masonry surface.

It is important to recognise and remedy any problems before you begin to decorate. The most common are outlined below.

EFFLORESCENCE

BLOWN RENDER

RUST STAINS

Caused by mineral salts within the masonry reacting with water and crystallising on the surface. Scrape away deposits and do not paint the wall until it has dried out thoroughly. When painting over an area that has had efflorescence, only use water-based paints as they will allow any remnants of moisture to dry through the painted surface.

The render layer on a wall may sometimes break away from its block base, making the wall surface very unstable. This is mainly caused by expansion and contraction of water trapped underneath (see Blown Bricks). Render tends to blow in localised areas and should therefore be removed and patch filled (see pages 190–191).

Caused by external metal fittings that have corroded and washed down the wall in the rain, causing an unsightly stain. May also be caused by old rusting nails or metal fragments below the paint surface that have bled through. To remedy, ferrous metal fittings should be painted and stains cleaned down and sealed with an oil-based undercoat.

BLOWN BRICKS

Caused by water, trapped below the brick surface, expanding and contracting with extreme changes in temperature, very gradually breaking down the brick. Remove flaky debris and stabilise before painting (see pages 188–189).

MOULD/ALGAE GROWTH

Often found in the small damp areas around leaking gutters or downpipes. Once established, mould growth can become very extensive and must be treated thoroughly before painting (see pages 188–189).

CRACKS

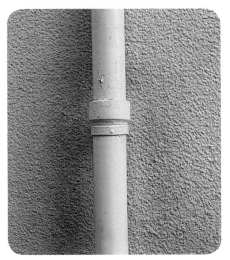

Caused by slight movement in the building. If extensive, cracking should be examined by a professional to check for major subsidence, smaller cracks can simply be filled with cement or exterior filler (see pages 190–191).

FLAKING PAINT

Caused by poor preparation when previously decorated or by water penetration. Must be scraped back to a sound surface before repainting (see pages 188–189).

ROTTEN WOOD

Caused by water, and by wood-eating pests. If extensive, replace entire section. In localised areas, cut away loose material, then treat and fill (see pages 192–193).

MORTAR DECAY

Damp and extreme temperature changes gradually break down the cement between blocks or bricks. Repoint before painting or damp proofing (see pages 206–207).

Paint and materials

It is always better to buy good-quality materials, as cheaper ones will not offer as much protection. Furthermore, having to add an extra coat of paint because you have chosen a low-cost, poor-covering alternative can lead to greater expense than if good quality paint had been purchased at first.

Here are most of the materials needed to carry out nearly all exterior painting work. As with tool purchase, be selective. For quantities of paint, check with both the table opposite and the product information on the back of the can.

BASIC SUPPLIES

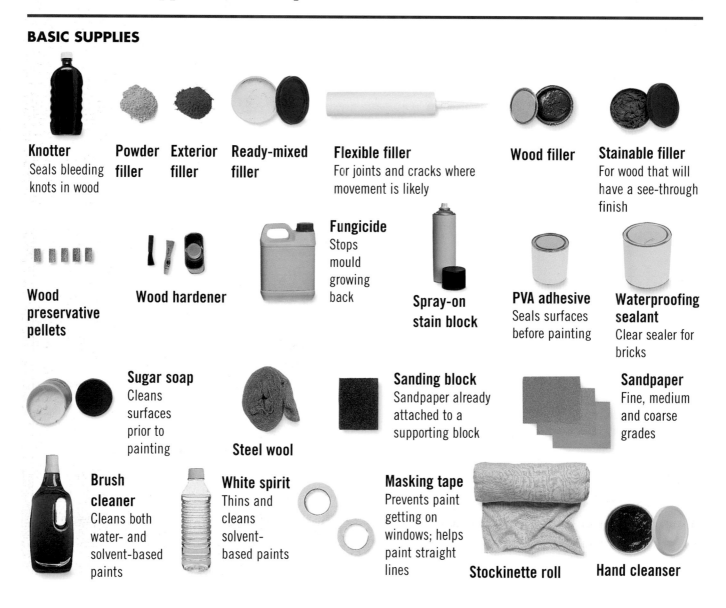

Knotter
Seals bleeding knots in wood

Powder filler

Exterior filler

Ready-mixed filler

Flexible filler
For joints and cracks where movement is likely

Wood filler

Stainable filler
For wood that will have a see-through finish

Wood preservative pellets

Wood hardener

Fungicide
Stops mould growing back

Spray-on stain block

PVA adhesive
Seals surfaces before painting

Waterproofing sealant
Clear sealer for bricks

Sugar soap
Cleans surfaces prior to painting

Steel wool

Sanding block
Sandpaper already attached to a supporting block

Sandpaper
Fine, medium and coarse grades

Brush cleaner
Cleans both water- and solvent-based paints

White spirit
Thins and cleans solvent-based paints

Masking tape
Prevents paint getting on windows; helps paint straight lines

Stockinette roll

Hand cleanser

Finishing

Primer, Undercoat

Paint, Stain, Varnish, Oil, Wood dye, Preservative

ACRYLIC/WATER-BASED

	sq m/litre	sq yd/gallon
Gloss	15	82
Primer/undercoat	10	55
Masonry paint (smooth surface)	12	65
Masonry paint (rough surface)	4	22
Wood stain	20	110

SOLVENT-/OIL-BASED

Gloss	17	92
Primer	20	110
Undercoat	15	82
Oil	12	65
Timber preservative	10	55
Varnish	16	87
Wood stain	22	120

CAUTION

Some materials contain hazardous chemicals. Always remember to read the manufacturers' guidelines before handling them.

COVERAGE

Try to be as accurate as possible when measuring the surface area of walls and treat each wall or aspect of a house separately. The width of a wall may be easily measured by simply running a tape measure along its base. To measure height on a two-storey building, pick a point by eye which is about half the total wall height, measure to this level and simply double it to gain the total height.

Use common sense when making deductions in surface area for windows and doors. Clearly there is no need to worry about making allowances for doors, but the dimensions of large picture windows should be deducted from the overall area.

Gaining accurate surface areas for windows can be more difficult. With casement windows composed of many small panes and rails, use the dimensions of the window to obtain a basic surface area. For windows that consist of a pane of glass and little more, make deductions for the glass.

Paint coverages are greatly affected by surface porosity. Obviously, unpainted render will require much more paint than a wall that was previously painted, and so before making a large purchase buy a small quantity of paint and test to see how far it will spread. The table above right is only an approximate guide for surfaces of average porosity.

MICROPOROUS PAINTS AND FINISHES

Many products have what are referred to as microporous properties. This means that they allow moisture to dry out through the finished surface, but do not allow moisture to penetrate back inwards.

These are clearly excellent preservative qualities and therefore such products are ideal for exterior decoration.

However, if you are using these products to recoat over a finish which does not have the same properties rather than applying them directly on to untreated surfaces, the microporous effect of the new paint is considerably diminished.

Masonry preparation

Because the walls are the largest surface area on the exterior of a house, they require the most paint and therefore incur the greatest expense. Most masonry paints have a guaranteed life expectancy of up to ten years, but without sound preparation their life can be at least halved. Good preparation is therefore vital, and the amount of work required depends largely on whether the walls have been previously painted.

TOOLS: Scraper, 100–150mm (4–6in) brush, goggles, gloves, stiff brush, pressure washer, dust sheets

MATERIALS: Fungicide, stabilising solution

1 On old or previously painted walls, use a scraper to get rid of any flaky paint or loose material. Anything growing on the walls, such as lichen, must be completely removed.

2 Check for any signs of mould or algae growth. This is most likely to be present on older, previously painted render, but may also be found on newer unpainted surfaces. Apply fungicide liberally to all affected areas with a large 100–150mm (4–6in) brush; check the manufacturer's instructions as it may require dilution before application. Wear safety goggles and gloves as the fungicide is toxic.

3 On exterior walls that have a thick, extensive growth of either mould or algae it may be necessary to use a stiffer brush in order to remove the deposits completely. Scrub the affected area very thoroughly. In such cases, more than one application of fungicide may be required to clear the surface.

4 Leave the wall for at least 24 hours to allow the fungicide enough time to kill off all traces of mould or algae. Then thoroughly wash down all areas with clean water. A pressure washer is ideal, as it both cleans off any traces of fungicide and dead algae as well as removing any loose material that may have been missed during step 1. When using a pressure washer always wear goggles for protection against flying debris.

6 Such areas must be treated with a stabilising solution to bind the surface together so that it is able to accept paint. Wear protective goggles and gloves and apply to all affected areas making sure that they are completely covered. Using stabilising solution has the added advantage of reducing the porosity of the masonry. Paint will therefore go much further than on an untreated surface. Make sure that all areas are covered with dust sheets and windows and doors are protected or masked as unwanted splashes are difficult to remove.

5 Once dry, check whether walls are sound and free from loose material of any nature. Some surfaces may still have a chalky or powdery texture from mortar/cement breakdown caused by general ageing.

Filling masonry

Cracks and holes in masonry should be filled in, not only to make the finish as attractive as possible, but also because it is necessary in order to close off any routes where water might penetrate into the wall, and thereby into the house, forming damp patches and spoiling the interior decoration.

While modern masonry paint will cover up and seal hairline cracks, anything larger must be cleaned out and filled. Always use filler specifically designed for exterior use as all-purpose fillers are not sufficiently durable to withstand the harsh effects of weathering.

TOOLS: Dusting brush, filler board, filling knife, 50mm (2in) brush, sponge, bucket, hawk, plastering float

MATERIALS: Exterior filler, cement, sand, jug of water, mortar plasticiser/ household detergent, PVA adhesive

SMALL CRACKS

1 The crack must be freed of any loose debris such as small pieces of mortar, grit and cobwebs. If the material is very hard to shift, you may need to use a scraper, but most dirt can be cleaned out with a dusting brush.

2 Pour the required amount of exterior filler on to a filler board. Old paint-tub lids make excellent boards as they have a rim to prevent water pouring off, and as they are made of plastic they are easy to keep clean. Make a small depression in the centre of the filler with a filler knife and add water gradually, mixing into a wet, pliable consistency.

3 Use a small brush to wet the crack with water. This helps the filler to bond with the masonry and slows down the drying time, reducing the risk of shrinkage or cracking.

4 Use a filling knife to firmly press the filler into the crack, smoothing the surface as you go. Try to remove any excess filler from around the crack while the filler is still wet.

5 Wipe over the filler with a damp sponge. This reduces the need for sanding once it is dry which is difficult as exterior filler is coarser and harder than interior or all-purpose filler.

LARGE HOLES

1 For larger holes, or areas of blown render, a sand–cement mix should be used for patching. Initially, mix dry in a ratio of 5 parts sand : 1 part cement. Add water gradually and mix to a wet, stodgy consistency. Add mortar plasticiser or a little household detergent to improve the workability of the mix.

2 Remove any loose debris from the hole and wet the area as covered in steps 1 and 3 above. A small quantity of PVA adhesive mixed with the water (1 part PVA : 5 parts water) will aid the bonding process between the mix and the wall surface. Transfer the cement mix to a hawk and use a plastering float to press the mix into the hole. This is often a messy process, so by holding the hawk below the area being filled, it is possible to catch the excess.

3 Smooth the surface of the wet render, matching it with the surrounding area. Allow it to dry slightly, then use a wetted float to polish the surface. You may need to repeat this if necessary. If the patch starts to bulge, this usually means the hole is too deep to fill in one go. Take back the patch to below the wall level, allow to dry and apply a second layer of the render mix.

Woodwork preparation

By nature, wood is less hard-wearing than masonry and therefore requires more frequent attention. Even the highest quality paints will rarely last longer than five years on wood, making sound preparation essential (see pages 40–41).

Problems caused by weathering, including wet and dry rot and damaged, flaking paintwork must be dealt with prior to painting. Before applying any paint, thoroughly clean all the surfaces with a solution of sugar soap or household detergent and rinse them down with clean water.

TOOLS: Bucket, sponge, scraper, dusting brush, electric drill, 15mm (½in) paintbrush, gloves

MATERIALS: Sugar soap, household detergent, wood filler, wood hardener, preservative pellets, filler, sandpaper, primer

FILLING WOOD

Filling and sanding wood surfaces not only makes them look good, but also encourages water to run off, preventing damage. All-purpose powder fillers are ideal for small nicks and holes, while flexible filler is used for cracked panels or areas where movement between different parts of the joint is likely (see pages 42–43).

Specialist wood filler is ideal for large holes or areas that have been treated for rot. These fillers are usually supplied as a thick paste which needs to be mixed with a hardening compound just before application.

ROTTEN WOOD

1 Where the wood has rotted in small, localised areas it must be removed and the area filled. With a scraper, cut loose or decaying wood back to sound dry timber. When all the rot has been removed, dust away loose debris.

2 Apply some wood hardener to the bare wood. This is usually made up by mixing a hardening compound with another chemical solution, so follow the manufacturer's guidelines carefully. Saturate the affected area with the hardener.

3 As a further precaution to prevent rot from spreading, preservative pellets may be used. Drill a series of holes around the rotten area about 75mm (3in) apart. In the example shown here, it would be wise to progress along the entire length of the window sill.

4 Push a preservative pellet into each hole. They will slowly release a chemical that impregnates and therefore protects the wood from further rot. Make sure each pellet rests below the surface of the wood. Seal the holes with wood filler, filling them proud and then sanding them down.

DAMAGED PAINTWORK

1 Less severely damaged areas must also be repaired. Where the old painted surface has blistered or flaked, use a scraper to remove all the unstable or loose material.

2 Sand the area of bare wood thoroughly, removing any loose pieces of paint or wood. Feather the edges of the sound paint in with the now bare area of wood.

3 Using a small brush – a 15mm (½in) brush is ideal for windows – prime the bare patch of timber, slightly overlapping the primer on to the surrounding painted wood.

Painting

To reap the rewards of careful preparation to the full, it is very important to use the correct techniques for applying paint. Refer to the relevant sections in Chapter 1, Painting Interiors for instructions on the correct techniques for preparing paint and using a roller, brush and sprayer.

As a general rule, start at the top of the house and work down. Fascias and guttering should be painted first, followed by the walls, followed by windows and doors. Leave any smaller accessories, such as outside lights or metal-work until last. Keeping to a logical order like this will avoid having to repeat any task unnecessarily.

Only undertake painting when the weather is fine. Bad weather – even small sprinklings of rain – may not only reduce the paint's preservative qualities but also ruin the decorative finish, while painting in direct sunlight speeds up drying times and makes the paint harder to spread.

Textured coatings

Coatings with an in-built texture give a hard-wearing, decorative finish and are becoming increasingly easier to apply to most prepared masonry surfaces. Although they tend to be expensive, they are durable enough to outlast any standard paint treatment.

There are two main types. Tyrolean is a coarse finish that uses a hand-held machine to splatter the coating on to the wall. Alternatively, various proprietary coatings are applied with a trowel, float, roller or even a sprayer, and then textured with a range of special tools.

TOOLS: Hawk, metal float, 25–37mm (1–1½in) paintbrush, sponge, bucket, textured roller, texture tools

MATERIALS: Textured coating, water

SURFACES AND REQUIREMENTS

Ideally, a textured coating should be applied direct to rendered walls that have been prepared thoroughly (see pages 188–189). Most walls made from facing bricks and building blocks are also suitable, as long as their pointing is flush with the bricks or blocks.

Some manufacturers will insist that a plinth be provided at the level of the damp-proof course. Always check the manufacturer's guidelines before starting to use a textured coating, and carefully mask up all areas before application.

COVERING CRACKS

Textured coatings are also useful for covering small cracks on a rendered surface. Larger cracks can initially be filled with the textured coating instead of filler and then a top coat applied.

1 A textured coating may be applied with a roller or, as shown here, using a metal float and hawk. Applying a texture is an ideal job for two people as one can float on the coating while the other follows behind, making the texture in the surface.

2 To start with, apply a layer 1–2mm (¹⁄₁₆ in) thick, in areas of 1–2sq m (1–2½sq yd) at a time, taking care to smooth the surface and ensuring coverage is even. Where possible, finish coating at a natural break, as it dries quickly.

3 One way to produce a decorative finish is to run a textured roller across the surface of the coating. Then float more coating on to the next adjoining area and repeat the texturing process, keeping a wet edge going at all times.

4 In awkward or small areas where the roller will not go, such as cutting in around windows or behind downpipes, dab a small paintbrush in the coating to produce the required textured effect.

5 There are many different types of texturing tool that can be used to create a variety of effects. Always practise producing a consistent pattern before you commit yourself to covering a large area.

6 Keep washing tools in clean water during application as drying paint will hinder progress. Finally, remove any masking immediately after the texturing is complete as it will be difficult after the coating has dried.

Guttering and fittings

Keeping the external fixtures and fittings of a house, such as guttering, downpipes or other metallic accessories, in good decorative order, not only prolongs their life but also enhances the rest of the exterior decoration.

The sole purpose of guttering is to channel water away from the house and it is therefore the exterior fitting that receives the greatest amount of attack from water. It is important to keep it in a sound condition to protect the rest of the house.

TOOLS: Bucket, sponge, trestles, filler dispenser, 25–50mm (1–2in) paintbrush, fitch, wire brush

MATERIALS: Paint, gutter sealant, sugar soap, piece of card, white spirit, cloth, aerosol spray paint, proprietary metal paint

METAL GUTTERING

2 Use a fitch to reach inaccessible areas that must be painted to prevent damage. It is also ideal for cutting in around the brackets.

1 Cast-iron guttering is difficult to take down for painting, due to its weight, and because lengths tend to be bolted together and sealed at the joints. Therefore, removal could be a long process resulting in resealing every joint when replacing the gutter, so paint it in position. Painting inside the gutter will sustain its life, make water run-off more efficient and reduce the risk of loose material building up, causing blockages. Proprietary metal paints are ideal for all metal guttering except aluminium.

3 To prevent any splashes of paint getting on to a newly painted wall, when painting the back of downpipes, hold a piece of cardboard behind the pipe in order to shield the wall.

PLASTIC GUTTERING

Plastic guttering is popular because it is simple to maintain. It can be easily unclipped and removed and, unless old and discoloured by the sun, needs only to be cleaned down with a sugar-soap solution before being replaced. To repaint, simply apply one or two coats of gloss directly to the cleaned-down surface.

Leaks tend to occur on joints between lengths. In problem areas, unclip the joint, dry all surfaces, then run a bead of gutter sealant around the affected area and clip the gutter back together. Remove any excess sealant quickly with a cloth dampened in white spirit.

ASBESTOS GUTTERING

As it is considered a health risk, ideally guttering made from asbestos should be replaced. However, if you do decide to paint it, wear protective clothing, which must include a respiratory mask. Never sand asbestos as the dust caused is dangerous if breathed in. If you have to remove any flaky paint, damp the paint, then carefully remove the loose flakes with a scraper.

A water-based paint is the best choice for painting asbestos guttering, as it may be applied direct to the surface and its permeability allows the surface of the asbestos to breathe, reducing the risk of the paint blistering. If you wish to paint the guttering with an oil-based gloss, prime any bare patches with an alkali-resistant primer.

METAL FITTINGS

Before painting a ferrous metal such as cast iron, use a wire brush to remove any loose, flaky material. Then apply one or two coats of a proprietary metal finishing paint directly on to the bare and previously painted metal surface. Primers are not required with this type of finishing paint. When using other types of paint, check the manufacturer's guidelines as some metal surfaces will require specific primers.

EASIER PAINTING

It is often easier to take down small metal fittings for painting. An intricately designed object, such as a hanging basket bracket, can be painted very quickly using aerosol spray paint. Spray such items on a wooden board which acts as a non-stick surface while the object is drying.

Always follow the manufacturer's instructions on the can when using spray paints. Avoid contact with eyes or skin. These paints are also highly inflammable: keep away from heat and dispose of the cans safely.

External doors

Exterior doors bear the brunt of the elements, such as sun and rain, plus added wear from frequent opening and closing, making them even more liable to cracking joints, knocks and dents. In addition, the front door tends to be a focal point in the appearance of the house and so achieving the best finish possible should be a priority.

Take time to ensure you carry out the task correctly and bear in mind that, because of unavoidable wear and tear, doors may need painting more regularly than other areas.

TOOLS: Trestles, dust sheet, 37mm (1½in) paintbrush, 50mm (2in) paintbrush

MATERIALS: Paint

PANELLED DOORS

1 Front doors are usually more solid than internal doors, in order to stand up to the demands asked of them. However, without care they will deteriorate quickly and are expensive to replace, so always pay particular attention to hidden areas such as underneath the weather board at the bottom. Water can seep up through this area if unprotected.

2 Before painting the door, remove it from its hinges and lay it on trestles. Work upwards from the bottom of the door, starting with the weather board. Apply knotter if necessary, primer-undercoat and gloss. By using water-based paint, this operation can be completed in a day so that the door can be replaced before nightfall.

3 Drips and runs of wet paint are always a problem when painting vertical surfaces, in particular where there are protruding panels or corners where paint can collect. So, once you have finished painting the door, return to it at regular intervals during the drying time to remove any drips or runs that may have formed.

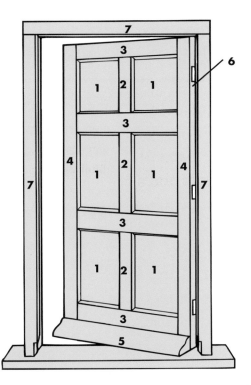

ORDER OF WORK

This diagram shows both the best sequence in which to paint a panel door and where the dividing line is between the interior and exterior.

1 Panels, working from left to right and downwards.
2 Central stiles, from the top downwards.
3 Members from top downwards.
4 Hanging stile, then locking stile.
5 Weather board.
6 Hanging edge.
7 Frame.

To get access to all the door edges, and to reduce the risk of interruption due to rain and the problem of dust and insects getting on the newly painted surface, open the door inwards before painting. Remove all accessories, such as handles and door knockers, before painting.

If possible, do not paint the hinges as the paint will crack and flake away very quickly.

FLUSH DOORS

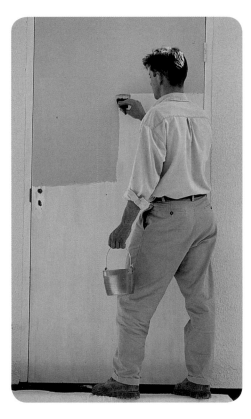

1 Mentally divide the door into eight sections. Begin by painting in the top left-hand corner, then move to the right and downwards. A 50mm (2in) brush is ideal for this job. Take care not to overload the wet edges of each section as this can easily lead to paint runs and sagging.

2 Continue to paint the door, working on one section at a time. Finish off the job by painting the door frame and the edges of the door, using a smaller brush.

PRESERVING DOOR SILLS
If wooden door sills are painted, they will be damaged quickly with chips and scuffs caused by people walking over them. It is more successful to treat them with a wood preservative or stain that can better absorb wear and tear.

Casement windows

Shapes and sizes of casement windows vary, but they are a very common type of window.

Make sure that all opening casements (lights) are partially open to allow movement, and access to edges and internal rebates. Check that these often neglected areas have been cleared of cobwebs and dust during preparation.

Paint casement windows in a logical sequence to save time on what could otherwise be a painstaking procedure. It is also best to paint them early in the day so that there is plenty of time for the paint to dry before the windows are closed in the evening.

TOOLS: 25mm (1in) paintbrush, 25mm (1in) angle-headed paintbrush, paint kettle

MATERIALS: Paint

1 Begin with the smallest opening light, painting the edges and frame rebates. Allow the light to remain slightly open to avoid sticking.

2 Paint the putty or glazing beads surrounding the window panes. A 25mm (1in) angle-headed brush makes it easier to apply the paint right into the corner of the frame.

Bead the paint up to the glass edge, overlapping very slightly on to the glass to create a sealed edge. Paint the central glazing bar at the same time.

3 Finish this first opening light by painting the horizontal rails, and then the vertical rails. Take care that paint does not run down to the bottom of the light, making it hard to close later.

4 Repeat the same sequence of steps with the large opening casement or light, again making sure that it is not closed once painted, to avoid sticking.

METAL AND PVC WINDOWS

On metal windows that are normally painted, clean back any patches of rust to sound, bare metal and then treat with metal primer. Once this has been done, prepare and paint in exactly the same way as their wooden counterparts.

Aluminium and PVC windows are specifically designed to require very little maintenance and should not require painting. If weathering has taken its toll, a wash down with warm, soapy water should return the frames to a clean, bright condition. Never use abrasive cleaners as they may scratch the surface.

5 Paint the sealed casement. There are no edges to worry about here, so begin with the putty or beads followed by the glazing bars, and work out to the horizontal and vertical rails.

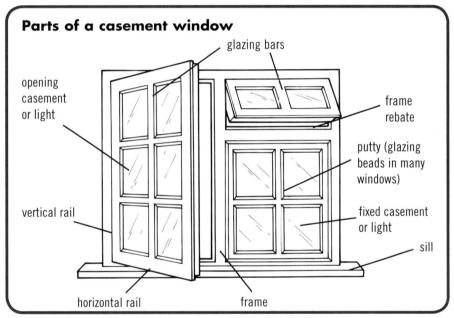

Parts of a casement window

glazing bars

opening casement or light

frame rebate

putty (glazing beads in many windows)

vertical rail

fixed casement or light

sill

horizontal rail

frame

6 Paint the frame. You may need to open the casements to do this, before returning them to a position just ajar.

7 Finish off by painting the window sill, being sure to paint the underside. Most sills have a small groove or drip guard stretching the length of the underside to prevent water running back to the wall where it may penetrate between the wood and masonry. Therefore, make sure that this groove is clear of obstruction and that there is not too much paint build-up along it, which would reduce its effectiveness.

Sash windows

Due to their design, sash windows appear to be difficult to paint, but if the correct sequence of painting is followed, they are as straightforward as any other job. If the runners are sound and no colour change is required, they should not be repainted as too many coats of paint will make the window jam.

As with all windows, begin painting them at the start of the day so they are dry and ready to close at nightfall.

TOOLS: 37–50mm (1½–2in) paintbrush, fitch, paint kettle, window guard, window scraper

MATERIALS: Paint, sandpaper, all-purpose filler

Parts of a sash window exterior

outer sash

vertical rail

glazing bar

putty or glazing beads

frame

inner sash

horizontal rail

sill

runners

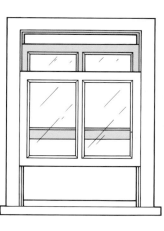

1 Lift the inner sash nearly to the top of the frame and lower the outer sash to about half way down the frame. Paint the top half of the inner sash beginning with the putty or glazing beads, followed by the glazing bar, and then the vertical and horizontal rails, including the top edge of the upper horizontal rail. If required, paint the top sections of the external runners (see page 83).

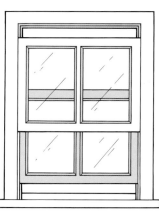

2 Lower the inner sash to a slightly open position and push the outer sash nearly to the top of the window frame. Finish painting the inner sash and begin to paint the outer sash, starting with the putty or glazing beads.

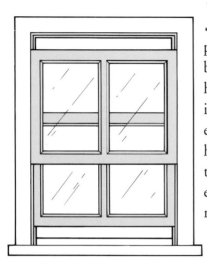

3 Complete the outer sash by painting the glazing bar, the vertical and horizontal rails, including the bottom edge of the lower horizontal rail. Paint the other half of the exterior runner, if needed.

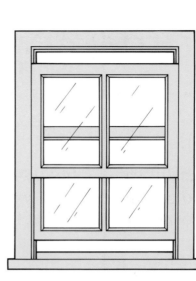

4 Finish the window by painting the window frame and finally the sill, including the underside and checking that the drip guard is clear (see page 203).

CORRECTING COMMON FAULTS

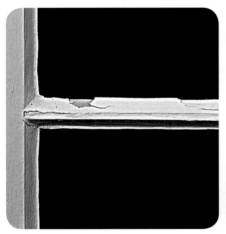

Lifting paint on putty

This is caused by painting the putty before it has completely dried out. Remove any flaky paint from the putty and sand the surface. If the damaged area of putty is basically sound, fill any cracks with an all-purpose filler, using a finger to apply it. When the filler is dry, sand down with a fine grade sandpaper, then repaint.

Blistering/bubbling

Occurs when moisture or air is trapped beneath the paint, (normally on wooden surfaces) and has expanded due to the heat caused by direct sunlight. Strip back, fill any holes if necessary and repaint. Bubbling may also be caused by painting directly on top of poorly prepared or dusty surfaces. Sand back, prepare correctly and repaint.

IDEAL TOOLS

Window scraper
Handy for removing paint overspill or spray from the glass of the window once the paint has dried.

Fitch
Useful for painting the runners as it is important to keep paint clear of the sash cord, otherwise the sliding mechanism will be hampered.

Waterproofing

Although they are not at all decorative, various waterproofing substances – all of which are painted on – are vital for exterior maintenance and decoration. These include liquid rubber for felt-covered flat roofs, clear waterproofing sealant for unpainted walls and flexible sealant for the gaps that may occur around window and door frames.

In spite of their limited decorative appeal, these products provide essential protection against water penetration, and are especially useful for surfaces that are particularly vulnerable to weathering. They have a longer lifespan than other painting products, so rest assured you will not have to use them every time you redecorate.

TOOLS: Stiff brush, old 50–75mm (2–3in) paintbrush, hawk, trowel, broom, gloves, respirator mask, goggles, filler dispenser, filler knife

MATERIALS: Cement and sand mix, waterproofing sealer, liquid rubber primer, liquid rubber, masking tape, frame sealant

WATERPROOFING AND SEALING WALLS

Clear liquid waterproofers do not change the appearance of the surface to which they have been applied. Paint can generally be applied over them if required (although a time lapse of weeks rather than days may be needed for application of water-based paints).

2 The quickest and easiest way to brush down an exterior wall, to remove any loose material, is to use an ordinary household broom.

1 Surfaces must be filled before waterproofing. Rake out any decaying mortar from between bricks and repoint using about 1 part cement : 6 parts sand mix. This mix will vary according to the exact surface; most building merchants will happily supply advice on composition.

3 Most types of waterproofing sealers are supplied in metal screw-top cans with a trigger spray and attachment that is easily connected to the spout of the can. This is an efficient method for applying the sealer, but if you are using it, be sure to wear protective gloves and a respiratory mask. On very porous surfaces, two coats will be required.

PREPARING FOR A NATURAL WOOD FINISH

Before deciding on which natural wood finish to apply – stain, wood oil or varnish – consider the preservative and decorative qualities that each offers (see page 177).

It is important to remember when buying preparatory materials for natural wood finishes that the translucent qualities of stains or varnishes have specific requirements. For example, they will not disguise filler unless it is specifically designed to match the wood or finish colour. Likewise, if repairing putty use a colour that closely matches the existing one, as standard white putty will not stain effectively to provide a match. Remember also that putty, generally, will not accept varnish.

TREATING KNOTS

Bleeding or seeping knots will often spoil a natural wood finish. To render them inactive, use a hot-air gun to draw the sap out of the wood, scraping away the residue until no more appears. Take care not to scorch the wood surface with the hot-air gun as it will spoil the eventual finish.

4 'Touch in' the bare areas of wood with a protective base coat if required (see pages 176–177). Allow it to dry and then touch in with the same coloured stain or varnish that was used on the previous decoration.

The old, sound coating will now be matched in with the newly coated bare areas and the surface will be ready for the required number of top coats (see pages 176–177).

REVIVING OLD WOOD

Where surface coatings have almost completely weathered away or the wood has become denatured and lacks colour, it is possible to breathe some life back into it before decoration. First, any areas of rot should be treated and filled in exactly the same manner as for painted surfaces (see pages 192–193) except the wood filler used must be stainable and able to receive a natural wood finish. Sand back the surface of the wood to remove any powdery or decaying material, and thoroughly rub in a coat of wood reviver.

WOOD STAINS

1 Most items have to be stained in position, but doors can be removed and stained flat on trestles. This avoids drips or runs and makes application far easier. Apply a base coat to the wood before staining, if recommended by the manufacturer.

2 Doors should be stained in the same order as for painting (see pages 200–201). Work in the direction of the grain, brushing the stain well into the surface. Do not overload the brush; this can result in uneven coverage.

3 Overlapping edges and brush strokes will show if not properly brushed out in the direction of the grain. Define each section with straight lines, never allowing a ragged edge to dry. Use the brush to 'pick up' any drips along the edges.

4 Lightly sand the surface with a fine grade sandpaper between coats, but not after the final coat. After each sanding, remove the dust and fine debris by wiping the surface down with a lint-free cloth dampened with a little white spirit.

5 The other advantage of taking the door off its hinges is that the underneath of the weather board and the bottom edge of the door can be stained as well. This protects them from the inevitable, and damaging, penetration of rainwater.

GETTING THE RIGHT RESULT

Although the effect of stains is usually stunning, a certain amount of care is needed during application to achieve the right result.

Always stain in the direction of the grain, brushing out well to avoid individual brush strokes showing when the stain is dry. Avoid overlapping edges of stain on the individual sections of the door and define them with straight lines. Use a brush to 'pick up' any drips along the edges.

VARNISHES

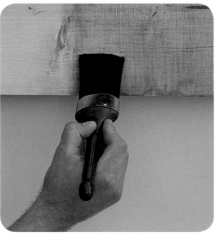

1 When varnishing bare wood it may be necessary to apply a protective base coat before the varnish itself. This is common when using solvent-based varnishes. When using some base coats, wear protective gloves.

2 If using a base coat, allow it to dry for the time specified by the manufacturer. Then apply the first coat of varnish, initially with vertical up-and-down strokes at right angles to the grain of the wood.

3 Before the vertical strokes begin to dry, immediately lay off the varnish with horizontal strokes in the direction of the grain. This method of vertical and horizontal brushing helps ensure total coverage.

WOOD OILS

1 Apply the oil liberally along the direction of the grain, saturating the wood completely. For outdoor furniture, soak the base of each leg to prevent water penetration.

2 Before the oil dries, remove any excess from the surface of the wood, by buffing it with a lint-free cloth. This polishes the surface, giving the finish a light sheen.

WOOD OILS

The colour range of wood oils is limited as the wood colour itself is relied upon to provide the decorative aspect of the treatment. Oil should be reapplied every one to two years to keep the wood in a highly decorative condition. This is not too arduous as it is very quick to apply and requires no base coat. Two coats of oil should be applied.

Oily rags are flammable and should be stored or disposed of safely by placing in a sealable, water-filled metal container. Always keep the container outside.

Fault finder

All manner of problems and faults may occur during painting or wallpapering or after the job has been completed. Most can be put down to hasty preparation, incompatible materials, or rushed work. Always remember to read the manufacturer's guidelines for specific paints and papers, and never try to cut corners. Some of the most common problems and ways to prevent and rectify them are outlined below.

POOR PAINT COVERAGE

Usually found where a solvent-based gloss has been applied over the wrong undercoat, or even no undercoat at all. Sand back and apply the correct paint that should have been used at first. With water-based paints, it is usually due to insufficient coats of paint. Adding extra coats will normally solve the problem.

MISCELLANEOUS STAINS

Damp patches, rust spots or bleeding bitumen are most often found 'grinning' through emulsion or water-based paints, as solvent-based paints will often cover such problems. Apply a stain block, allow it to dry, and repaint the surface. For persistent damp stains or unidentifiable marks, consult a professional.

ROLLER TRAILS

Occur in uneven areas because the roller is unable to run across the surface smoothly. They can also be caused by applying too much pressure to the roller while it is moving. Lightly sand back and repaint.

ORANGE PEEL/WRINKLING

Caused when a solvent-based paint has been applied over a first coat of paint that has not completely dried. Strip the paint back to the bare surface and repaint, allowing adequate drying time between coats.

DRIPS AND RUNS

Occur when too much paint has been used on a vertical surface. Allow the paint to dry completely, sand back to remove the runs and to get a smooth surface on which to work, then repaint.

BRUSH MARKS

Caused by general over application or lack of 'laying off' when painting. To solve the problem, the area must be sanded back completely or stripped, in severe cases. Then reapply the paint or stain.

BLISTERING/BUBBLING

Occurs when moisture or air is trapped beneath the paint and has expanded due to heat. Also occurs on poorly prepared surfaces. To solve the problem, strip back, fill any holes and then repaint.

POOR PAINT COVERAGE ON WOOD

Either caused by too few coats of paint or, more seriously, not having used a primer coat on the bare wood. Strip back to bare wood and prime before repainting correctly.

POOR PAINT COVERAGE ON MASONRY

Wall surface simply requires another coat of paint. Often occurs when trying to cover a dark colour with light or if paint has been poorly applied on a rough surface.

LIFTING PAINT ON PUTTY

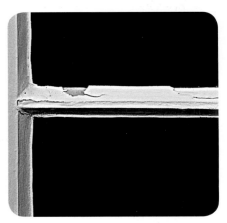

This is caused by painting the putty before it has completely dried out. Remove any flaky paint from the putty, fill any cracks with all-purpose filler, sand the surface, then repaint.

DAMP STAINS ON PAPER

Some damp stains will disappear once the wallpaper has been allowed to thoroughly dry out. With some heavy papers, this may take days. If they do not, strip the paper and treat the damp problem in the wall underneath.

SAGGING PAPER

Caused by too much pressure being applied with the paper-hanging brush during application, so that it stretches and creases the wet, pliable wallpaper. If the effect is too noticeable, stripping and repapering will be necessary.

OVERLAPPING/LIFTING SEAMS

Poor bonding on overlapping edges causes the paper to lift away from the wall surface. Use a fitch to apply some overlap adhesive. Then smooth the paper back into position with a damp sponge, removing any excess adhesive.

BUBBLING PAPER

Bubbles remaining when the paper is thoroughly dry are caused by trapped air and usually occur when the paper has not been soaked for long enough. Pierce the bubbles with a craft knife and stick the paper back, sponging off any excess adhesive. If the problem is extensive, strip the paper off and begin again.

WHITE SEAMS

Commonly caused by poor butt-joining or shrinkage while the paper was drying out. In minor instances, use a felt-tip pen or crayon of a similar colour to the base colour of the paper and carefully run down the affected seams. Some paper manufacturers provide special felt tips for exactly this purpose.

CREASES

Caused by poor technique or when stretching paper around an external corner that is not square. Remedy in a similar way to bubbling paper, piercing the bubbles with a craft knife and sticking the paper back with adhesive. If the problem is extensive, strip and re-hang the paper.

POOR PATTERN MATCH

Normally caused by poor application, in which case the only solution is to strip the paper and start again. Sometimes there is a variation in the degree to which the pattern matches along a seam.
More tolerance to this sort of imperfection is necessary if the paper is hand printed. In some cases, the paper may be from a faulty batch, so you should always check how well the pattern matches at the early stages of preparation (see pages 98–99).

STAINED SEAMS OR PASTE ON PAPER

If paste has dried on the surface of the paper this will often show, spoiling the decorative finish (especially on some matt wallpapers). This is caused by not wiping wet paste from the surface
during paper hanging. If the paper is washable try removing the paste with a sponge and a solution of mild detergent. Similar to this are shiny seams where the joins have been over brushed during application resulting in a polished effect. There is no remedy, so be less vigorous when you next hang wallpaper.

TORN PAPER

Caused by accidentally snagging the paper on something. A tear often looks devastating, but by carefully applying some overlap adhesive and pushing the paper back into place, most tears become invisible to the naked eye.

FLATTENED RELIEF

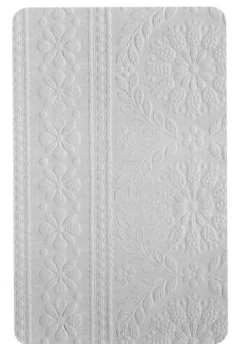

Caused by applying too much pressure, normally on embossed papers, when hanging. Never use a seam roller on such papers. Small areas should not be too noticeable; larger areas may need stripping and repapering.

Glossary

Acrylic
A fast drying water-based material used for paint finishes, drying to a tough waterproof finish.

Architrave
Decorative moulding surrounding a door or window which covers the join between the frame and the wall.

Barge boards
Boards attached to the rafters on the exterior of a house, at the gable end.

Batten
A length of straight wood, used as a guideline.

Beading
Using the extreme edge of a paintbrush to achieve a precise dividing line between two colours.

Biscuit
The clay body of a tile to which a liquid ceramic glaze is applied. The tile is then 'fired' under intense heat in a kiln to set the glaze into a very hard surface. Patterned tiles may be fired several times, each part of the pattern being added separately.

Bleeding
Paint that seeps under the edge of a stencil or from one surface to another.

Blitzer
Hand-held tool, which when pressed emits paint blown from the end of a felt tip.

Blown
Where the top layer of masonry has separated from the main block structure of the wall: eg cement render separating from a brick wall.

Border
A narrow, decorative band of wallpaper, stencilled designs or tiles.

Border tile
A narrow tile designed specifically for edging an area of tiles, usually with glazed outer edges to provide a neat finish.

Butt join
A join where two edges of wallpaper or lining paper meet exactly, but do not overlap.

Ceiling rose
An electrical fitting found on ceilings through which a lighting pendant hangs.

Centralisation
The process of centring the dominant part of the pattern in a wallpaper on a focal point in a room, such as the middle of a chimney breast.

Chalk line
A length of string covered in chalk dust, pulled tight and snapped against a surface to leave a straight guideline.

Complementary colours
Two colours from opposite sides of the colour wheel which enliven each other.

Concertina
Wallpaper or lining paper that has been folded into manageable lengths, usually after pasting.

Corner trim
A moulded plastic strip designed for finishing an external corner where two tiled walls meet.

Cure
Period of chemical change when paint hardens to provide a tough waterproof surface.

Cutting in
Painting into an angle such as between a wall or ceiling, or on to a narrow surface such as a glazing bar. Alternatively, cutting tiles to fit a narrow gap at the end of a row.

Dado
A decorative strip running horizontally across a wall at waist height.

Damp-proof course
A layer of impenetrable material placed at about 150mm (6in) above ground level to prevent moisture penetration.

Detack
Remove some stickiness from a surface. Masking tape should be applied to a clean fabric surface a number of times before it is applied to a wall or it can damage the wall surface when it is removed again.

Distemper
Old-fashioned water-based paint.

Double lining
Two layers of lining paper, used to achieve a smooth finish on a rough surface.

Dowel
A short round length of wood (ideal for stirring paint).

Eggshell
A durable oil-based, mid-sheen paint which is an ideal base for most glaze finishes.

External corner
A corner where two walls meet, that sticks out into the room.

Fascia
Lengths of board found just below the edge of the roof, used for attaching guttering.

Feathering
Blending in uneven edges during sanding.

Ferrule
The metal band on a paintbrush that holds the bristles on to the handle.

Field tiles
Standard, uncut tiles used to fill the central portion of a tiled area.

Flush
Term used to describe two level, adjacent surfaces.

Frieze
Similar to a border, a band of decoration usually applied horizontally to a wall.

Gauge rod
A wooden batten, marked off at intervals, used to determine where the horizontal and vertical rows of tiles will fall on the wall.

Grout
Fills the joints between tiles, providing a very hard finish.

Grout raker
A rigid-bladed tool for scraping out old cracked and discoloured grout prior to renewing the grout or removing a damaged tile.

Grout shaper
A plastic tool for giving a neat, slightly recessed finish to grout joints while the grout is still soft.

Guide marks
Chalk or pencil marks that aid positioning.

Hardwoods
Normally found as smooth, planed wood. Very durable and more expensive than softwoods. Most often used for exterior purposes. Common hardwoods include oak, teak and iroko.

Hawk
Square metal or wooden board with a vertical handle beneath. Used as a platform for holding plaster, cement, filler, or textured coatings.

Hopper
Paint reservoir on airless spray equipment.

Horizontal parallel
Line level with the ground.

Insert tile
A small square tile inserted at the point where the corners of four larger tiles would normally meet.

Inset tile
A standard-size tile with a central motif used to provide visual interest in a large expanse of single-colour tiles.

Internal corner
A corner that does not stick out into the room.

Key
A slightly rough surface that has been sanded to provide a bond for paint, paper or tiles.

Laying off
Light brush strokes, made in a similar direction, to eliminate brush marks left on a painted surface.

Linseed oil
The base for traditional oil-based paints and transparent oil glaze.

Lint-free cloth
A cloth, usually made of cotton, which does not moult fibres.

Manufactured butt join
The process of overlapping wall coverings, cutting through both layers of paper and removing the excess strips to create a flush butt join.

Mask
Apply protection around an area to prevent paint misting.

Members
Horizontal wooden struts that are part of a panelled door.

Metal finishing paint
A rust-inhibiting paint that requires no primer or undercoat.

Microporous
The property of a paint or stain that allows moisture out but not into the surface of wood.

Mitre
An angled cut, made when joining two lengths of border in order to change direction. It is usually a 45-degree cut used to form a 90-degree corner.

Nibblers
Used for breaking off small amounts of waste when making a cut-out in a tile or removing a narrow strip. Special narrow-jawed versions are available for working in a confined space.

Parallel
Two lines that always remain the same distance apart.

Pattern drop
The misalignment of a pattern match on wallpaper.

Pattern repeat
The length over which a pattern repeats itself on a length of wallpaper.

Pencil tile
A very narrow tile, not much wider than a pencil, with a rounded face normally used in conjunction with dado tiles.

Picture tiles
Groups of tiles that fit together to make a larger picture.

Pigment
Natural colour source.

Plumb line
Length of string to which a weight is attached, giving a vertical guideline.

Primary colours
Yellow, blue and red, from which all other colours may be mixed.

Primer
Thinned, specially formulated paint that seals and stabilises a surface before undercoat is used.

Profile gauge
A special tool for copying the shapes of objects and transferring them to tiles for cutting.

Proud
Protruding slightly from the surrounding surface.

PVA
A multi-purpose adhesive and additive, primarily used in decorating as a sealer and bonding agent.

Quadrant tile
A narrow rounded tile for fitting at the junction of a tiled splashback and a bath or basin.

Rails
The horizontal and vertical struts in a window.

Re-positioning spray adhesive
Low-tack spray glue that allows for re-positioning.

Ready-pasted paper
Paper that has had paste coated on it when it was made. The paste is reactivated by soaking the paper in water before it is hung.

Rebate
The part of a rail that is at right angles to the pane of glass.

Render
A semi-smooth coat of sand and cement applied over a rough wall to give it a more even, protective coating.

Rocker
A tool used to imitate wood grain when working with glaze finishes.

Seam roller
A small, narrow plastic, felt or wooden roller used to roll gently along wallpaper seams to ensure good adhesion.

Setting out
Marking the wall with the starting point for tiling and fitting guide battens.

Size
A stabilising compound applied to porous surfaces to seal them before paper hanging.

Soaking
Period of time for the wallpaper paste to soak into the paper.

Softwood
Normally supplied as either smooth or rough sawn. Cheaper and less durable than hardwoods. Used for all sorts of joinery, interior or exterior, such as windows or fascia boards. Common softwoods include white deal and spruce.

Solvent
A cleaning or thinning medium for paint.

Squeegee
Term used for grout spreader, tool used for spreading grout.

Stiles
Vertical struts that are part of a panelled door.

Stripping
Removal of old wallpaper from a wall.

Template
Pattern used as a guide when cutting out.

Tile file
A special file for cleaning up the edges of tiles after they have been cut. Some have both flat and curved faces, allowing straight and curved cuts to be dressed.

Tile scorer
A tool with a narrow, hardened, chisel-like blade for scoring the glaze of a tile prior to snapping it in two. Without this, it is impossible to produce a clean, straight break.

Tile spike
A pencil-like version of the tile scorer with a needle-like tip. Easier to use than the chisel type, since its tip will sit tightly against the edge of a steel rule for greater accuracy when scoring.

Varnish
A protective medium which may be water- or oil-based.

Wall–ceiling junction
The corner where a wall meets the ceiling.

Wallpaper trough
A specially shaped container designed to hold water, for the purpose of soaking ready-pasted wallpapers.

Index